We Don't Go Far
But We Do See Life

We Don't Go Far But We Do See Life

By Keith Harris

BANOVALLUM
BOOKS

Published in Great Britain in 2020
by Banovallum Books
an imprint of Mortons Books Ltd.
Media Centre
Morton Way
Horncastle LN9 6JR

www.mortonsbooks.co.uk

**BANOVALLUM
BOOKS**

ISBN 978 1 911658 16 0

Typeset by Kelvin Clements

Printed and bound by Gutenberg Press, Malta

This book is dedicated to the memory of Eddie Dunford, forty years a landlord of the Black Horse at Telham, my dear friend and companion.

Contents

Chapter 1

Saul Trader

I ALWAYS GOT bored over Christmas. After over-relaxing and over-eating, with one Queen live at the Hammersmith Odeon and the other one telling us about her annus horribilis, I'd had enough.

It was 1976 and I wiled away a few hours by making a list of ten things I wanted to do during my allotted three score and ten. It was a fantasy, many years before the phrase bucket list was coined. Number five on the list was: Explore the waterways of Europe in a Dutch barge. Somehow, seeing it written down on paper made it feel possible—though in reality there was little hope. I had been married for a year and was working as an insurance agent with the Liverpool Victoria Friendly Society, collecting penny-policy premiums for £75 a week. I hated the job; the only saving grace was that I could get away with working two-and-a-half days a week. With the rest of the time I opened a small model shop and that was the beginning of 25 years of self-employment.

With a bit of hard work and more than my share of good luck, in 1998 I was in a position to buy a replica Dutch Luxemotor. Saul Trader was built by R W Davis Ltd (RWD) at Saul Junction on the Gloucester and Sharpness Canal. It was designed and constructed under the auspices of the yard's then manager, Phil Trotter. He's still there now, by the way, but nowadays I suppose you'd call him by some fancy title like chief exec or managing director. Not that Phil would ever court such grandeur; he's Phil and he's The Master. All the donkey work in running the yard is now under the control of Scragg, who back then was fresh out of school and on work experience. He certainly got plenty of that under the fatherly, unforgiving guidance of Phil, whom he dubbed The Master.

The boat was built in 1990 for the owner of the yard, Darrell, who christened it Saul Trader as a play on words of the phrase sole trader. An old sailor's superstition decreed it bad luck to change the name of a ship, but this had seemingly not reached the continent, as every ship that changed hands over there seemed to be given a new name. Nevertheless, I was reluctant to tempt fate and Saul Trader had a certain *je ne sais quoi* about it. RWD had also built my narrowboat some years earlier and I'd got to know them all pretty well. Wat Tyler was completed at the end of August 1990, coinciding with the Inland Waterways national rally which was held that year in Gloucester Docks. Wat Tyler was exhibited alongside Saul Trader, at that time was still in primer with engine and propulsion but without any internal fittings. On the way back to the yard after the show, I was steering Wat Tyler when Saul Trader came powering past, driven by Phil in his typically non-PC approach, doing at least 12 knots and causing a small tidal wave to wash the feet of the fishermen and carry away their keep nets.

The yard was full of characters and I often wished I'd had the time and the ability to write a sit-com about the crazy things that went on. It would have made Only Fools and Horses look more like Mrs Dale's Diary! There was Fat Keith, the mechanic. 'What do you think this is Phil, Howard's fucking Way?' he said once, after being asked to fit some stainless steel cleats. Keith once spent several days cramped into a tiny space in the corner of the engine room on Wat Tyler sorting out the Perkins diesel-fired central heating boiler. Most of the time was spent cursing and swearing at it until it finally burst into life, sending thick black clouds of smoke belching across the yard.

'How the hell does he ever get out of there?' I asked Phil, over the sound of a continuous stream of blasphemy emanating from inside the boat.

'That's simple is that,' Phil replied. 'Just tell him it's five to four.'

One of the fabricators, Paul, spent his weekends playing soldiers in the Territorial Army. He'd then spend most of the week boring everyone to death with stories of make-believe gallantry. He would demonstrate exactly how he'd shot half a dozen terrorists brandishing a piece of steel in lieu of a submachine gun and spraying the workshop with bullets shouting 'Dah dah dah dah dah! You're dead mate!' He once complained about one of his Saturday night compatriots: 'He don't take shots—I got him twice, but he wouldn't go down.'

There was a mechanic who stayed for a couple of years. John had worked in Bristol for British Aerospace, allegedly maintaining Rolls Royce engines. Whenever a plane flew overhead, he would stand and look up, cup his hand to an ear and announce: 'That sounds like one of mine.' He left the yard to work for a washing machine repairer. A few months later, he paid his old workmates a visit. He was sitting in Phil's office when the ancient machine used to wash the boiler suits started to clatter and bang and seemed on the point of exploding into fragments, potentially sending bits of underpants and boiler suits across the room. Without hesitation, Phil cupped his hand to his ear and said, 'Ay up John, that sounds like one of yours.'

One of the young gofers, a skinny lad with a look of neglect about him, acquired the nickname Runt. His claim to fame was that he had confused the brake with the throttle on the dumper truck and driven it over the edge of the wharf, coming to rest precariously balanced over the canal.

Then there was the inimitable Sean (Paddy) Care, whose talent for hand–painting boats was unmatched. Paddy did a beautiful job on Wat Tyler, but Phil complained that he always took too long. A lovable sort, Paddy was a little too sociable when it came to the pub and spent most of his evenings in The Three Horseshoes at the far end of Frampton village green, apparently the longest village green in England. He would then ride home on his bicycle, regularly falling off into the ditch and once even breaking his arm. Phil said he was lucky the ground broke his fall!

When he left the yard to work at a chipboard factory in Gloucester, he asked Phil for a reference. The first one Phil produced read something like: 'Sean is an extremely sociable fellow as any of the regulars in all the local pubs will testify. He doesn't do a very good job, but he always takes his time over it. He has a wonderful sense of logic and will paint the offside of a boat, balancing on the gunwale before methodically turning it round to do the other side. Sean is very keen and often takes work home with him in the evenings; he can often be seen walking home with a bundle of our best mahogany under his arm. His time keeping cannot be faulted—he is in the pub at 5.30 on the dot and never leaves before eleven. He is a very enterprising young man and has built up a lucrative trade in "imported" tobacco. Sean is always trying—often to the point of exasperation.'

Needless to say, a revised reference was produced, and Sean got the new job. On another occasion when they were launching a narrowboat, Runt unfortunately managed to leave his foot in a vulnerable place and got his toe caught under one of the rollers. The following day Sean arrived with a version of the 1960s song Big Bad John, re-written as Big Bad Toe: 'That big old boat came rollin' out and ran right over his toe. Big bad toe oh big bad toe.'

The sign writing was done by another colourful pair, Graham and Ann, who were from Romany stock and lived on a boat just down the canal at Fretherne. The longest serving employee was Stuart, who had been at the yard since the days when it was still owned by the Davis family. Stuart had never taken a day off in all his time there. I was told that every year he had a week's holiday and would take his family to Barrow Hill. 'Where's that?' I asked, thinking it might be somewhere warm and exotic. 'Over there,' Phil pointed. 'See that bit of a mound—that's Barrow Hill.' It was about half a mile from the boatyard, probably 150ft high, and apparently afforded some pleasant views across the Severn to the Forest of Dean on a clear day.

Scragg, the young apprentice, was actually christened Craig; I think it was me who gave him the nickname. At any rate, I was the only one who could get away with calling him Scragg—he got touchy about it as he grew older and was given more responsibility. He first came to the yard on a work experience week aged 15, and at 16 he started full-time. I don't think he ever contemplated working anywhere else. Scragg was brought up in

Stonehouse, about five miles from Saul. He hadn't travelled much, and he liked to play the part of the country
boy but in fact he had a worldly knowledge and a quirky
sense of humour. He also had a phraseology all of his
own and a unique sense of insight into people's foibles
and idiosyncrasies.

Scragg would come with us on the narrowboat two or
three times a year and, as far as I know, was the originator
of the descriptive phrase 'Wank Real Shit'—particularly
used when we spotted any vessel he deemed to be of
an inferior breed. He could identify boats from some
distance. 'That's a Broom 28—they're wank', he'd declare.
Or—'Just look at that fucking bow—that is wank.' Alter-
natively, anything he regarded as proper would be a beast,
pronounced as though the word was spelt with several 'e's.
'We've just started building a new barge—beeeeeast.' The
proud owner of one of their Northwich Trader narrowboats was obviously impressed as he actually called his
boat Beast, although spelt with just the one 'e'.

Over the years Scragg learned each aspect of boat-build-
ing—from fabrication and welding to joinery, painting,
mechanics and plumbing—from Phil, who he always
called The Master. I don't think he could have got a better
all-round education anywhere else, and he's still there
and still learning. He was dark-haired and slim and as
strong as an ox. A lot of girls found him attractive, but he
lacked a bit of confidence in those days and consequently
became entangled with several totally unsuitable women.

For a time, he lived in a dilapidated mobile home at the back of the yard and was pestered by a strange young lady with funny eyes who worked in the local garage, where he invariably bought his lunch usually consisting of a garage-brand pie and a Kit Kat. 'I got a stalker,' he told me with a grin one day. 'She won't leave me alone. She don't understand piss off and keeps sending me messages. That's textual harassment, that is.'

I had known Scragg for 12 years or so and we had done quite a lot of boating together on the English canals. He always looked forward to our next bit of 'croooosing'. For my 60th birthday, he and Phil presented me with a heavy ashtray hewn from a solid chunk of Gloucestershire stone and carved by the stonemason at Gloucester Cathedral, with three grooves set in to the top. Between the grooves in Roman-style lettering are the words 'Wank Real Shit!'

Phil—master boatbuilder, with a wonderful eye for the finished lines of a vessel—oversaw most of the work. He had joined the company a few years earlier, having been in partnership with Mike Adkins at Stoke on Trent Narrowboats, another builder of top-quality craft. Phil says he started out constructing boats in narrowboat builder David Piper's back garden. He survived a number of marriages and always said the only possessions he needed would have to fit into the boot of a Volkswagen Golf, ready for the next exodus. Mind you, he has a collection of more than 20 motorcycles, so a ten-ton truck would more likely be required. Saul is a wonderful backwater in a delightful area between the M5 and the meandering River Severn. Phil took to it all like the proverbial duck and settled in well with the characters and the ambience of the place. He has now been married to his lovely wife Annie for many years and has swapped the Golf for a Ford Ranger pick-up truck. I don't think he's got any plans to move out in the near future.

Saul Trader was based on a Dutch Luxemotor and Phil travelled to Zutphen in Holland to make drawings for a replica. It is 70ft long and 13ft in the beam. The interior is fitted out in Afromosia and teak. Afromosia is grown in West Africa and is sometimes known as African Teak because it has a very similar colour and grain. I like it for its smooth feel and luxurious sheen. This work was done by a guy called Rod who used bamboo saws, smoked strange-smelling cigarettes and considered his work an art. Rod worked for several years fitting out yachts at Falmouth. He only stayed at Saul for a couple of years, during which time he fitted out just two boats—Saul Trader and my narrowboat, Wat Tyler. The accommodation is a large double-back cabin with a beautifully rounded and panelled raised bed area right aft, a large engine room, lounge and galley, master bedroom and two further berths in a forward cabin. Each cabin had its own bathroom and shower (so basically three toilets equals three times more trouble!) The main engine is a six-cylinder Ford CS6, marinised by Lister. And there is an 8-kva Lister generator and heavy-duty battery charger, and diesel-fired central heating. Phil said there was enough power to run a small fairground.

I refer to the boat as it because a barge is an 'it'. I don't think a barge, as beautiful as it might be, can possibly be a she. Maybe a he perhaps—but that conjures up images of Fred Dibnah types with cloth caps and dirty boiler suits describing steam traction engines with names like Goliath or Majestic. No, I'm sorry if I am offending the romantic but a barge—a Dutch Luxemotor to boot—has got to be an it.

I bought it in 1998 and thought it was a bargain. As Phil once said about smuggled tobacco, 'it was so cheap you couldn't afford not to smoke.' I suppose you can't go far wrong if you buy something that has been built for the owner of the company. I had always assumed that, when buying a boat, traditionally you got what you saw, including the inventory. Not so with Darrell—he had stripped it bare! It was like buying a house and finding that the previous owners had taken the taps, light fittings and electrical sockets with them. It meant we had to start from scratch and chose all the crockery, utensils and bed linen to suit, but it cost the two days I'd planned for a shakedown trip on the canal. Maybe Darrell realised he'd let it go too cheaply and was trying to make a bit back. Well, it was still a bargain and I had no hard feelings but to set the record straight, several years later Darrell was shocked to learn that everything had been removed. He insisted he had left it all in situ and blamed his brother-in-law.

At that time the Cotswold Canals Trust held an annual festival at Saul, and I was delegated the job of musical director; it sounds grander than it actually was. We dubbed the festival Folk On The Water. I had always had a keen interest in the folk scene since the 1960s when I first heard Bob Dylan songs sung by a weird guy in the upstairs room of the Lord Nelson in Hastings. I was about 15 years old and spent my Sunday evenings with an illegal pint of warm bitter in the smoky atmosphere of the Old Town Folk Club. In the early 1990s, I had been mooring Wat Tyler outside a wonderful canal-side pub in Warwick called the Cape of Good Hope. Every Friday evening, they had a small folk session in the back bar and that's where I got friendly with one of the singers, Ron Holmes. Ron had a narrowboat called Tam Lyn (a Fairport Convention song), and he pointed out how both our boats were named after songs by the folk-rock band; they recorded a song about the 14th century rebel Wat Tyler in the late 1980s.

One day I visited the yard to see how work on the narrowboat was progressing and saw that Wat Tyler had been chalked on the bare steel by one of the boatyard wags. Maggie Thatcher was about to introduce the poll tax and apparently one of the fabricators (I think it was Paul) had been ranting that no way was he going to pay, and he would rather go to gaol or the gallows etc, etc. This prompted the inscription and I immediately realised this was going to be the name of the boat. Over the years it has attracted a variety of remarks, the most frequent being 'Ee was a Tolpuddle Martyr wasn't 'ee?' To which we'd reply, 'No—he was a revolting peasant.'

Ron had formed a duo with a songwriter guitarist from Stratford-upon-Avon, Allen Maslen, and they named themselves after Fairport's anthem, Meet On The Ledge. The festival director at Saul, Clive Field, knew of my interest in folk and asked me to organise some music. 'Couldn't we get that Sandy Denny bloke?' he asked, 'his stuff's brilliant!' At the first festival in 1999, we had a tent the size of a phone box and three bands. In fact, I think there were more musicians than audience. Meet On The Ledge topped the bill and went down a storm. In the afternoon I took them on the canal in Saul Trader. Ron and Allen sat on the foredeck with their guitars and Ron sang a lovely song written by Wolverhampton-based songwriter John Richards, called Honour and Praise:

On a fine summer's morning we lay at the quay
Our holds were filled high with the treasures of the sea
So that they could be transported by men such as we
To homeland and to Queen
When the loading was done, we hoisted full sail
Prayed for good winds to guide us and deliverance
  from gale
And the thoughts of the crew turned to home and
  strong ale
As we cast off the ropes and set sail

Fight for honour and for praise
Sail the sea throughout me days
In cold ground I'll never lay
I'd rather die on the ocean.

In the festival's early days, Saul Trader became a sort-of green room for performers to relax before gigs, and I felt very privileged to get to know some of them as friends. In 2006 we attracted some 12,000 people, put on more than 100 acts on three stages and made £50,000 for trust funds. We also had more people on the committee than who actually attended that first event! On one occasion we had the fantastically talented Old Rope String Band, led by Pete Chaloner. The performance comprised a lot of fooling about combined with a lot of excellent musicianship. One of their acts involved a game of tennis, with violins making the sound of the imaginary bat hitting the imaginary ball. At one point the ball veered off into the crowd and landed on the head of someone in the audience. Pete asked the unfortunate to kindly throw it back and the tennis resumed. At the end of the tune, Pete asked for a cheer for the reluctant hero with the words 'Ladies and gentlemen—big hand for this gentleman—what a tosser!' I was roped in as a stooge for another part. At a given signal from Pete, I had to rush on to the stage with a piece of paper and interrupt the performance to announce there was a vehicle on fire in the car park. As instructed, I read out the registration plate two or three times and, of course, there was no reaction. I then repeated 'Victor Hotel Romeo 729—a white Transit van', at which point Pete and fiddler Jo Scurfield dashed off stage in a cloud of dust leaving the third member, Tim, to recount some shaggy dog tale about his favourite childhood teddy bear. After about ten minutes Pete and Jo returned, their shirts torn, and faces charred with soot! Tragically Jo was killed some months later by a hit-and-run driver in Newcastle, and the band never recovered.

Another band that made a big impact were The Rollin' Clones tribute. Their last number was You Can't Always Get What You Want and the singer, Mark, recruited several young ladies onto the stage to join in the chorus. At the end as they were cheered off, Mark stood at the top of the steps and presented each of the girls with a mini Mars Bar—a nice touch. A few years later, an excellent band called Bluehorses made a live DVD recording at the festival, performing a version of the Deep Purple classic but renaming it Folk On The Water. After an arousing chorus of applause for an amazing solo, the lead singer and electric fiddler, Cardiff-born Lizzie Prendergast—thigh-length boots, short skirt and long black hair —sidled sexily up to the microphone, and said in her sultry voice, 'Classically trained, see.'

Bob Fox, who has made a bit of a name for himself as the song man in the War Horse productions, had his set interrupted when a bull jumped into the canal and started swimming frantically to Sharpness. When I asked Bob to do another appearance a few years later he said, in his inimitable Wearside, 'Only if you'll get that bull to lollop into the cut again.' Among other notable performances was Sid Kipper, who stopped mid-song and refused to go on unless a certain member of the audience turned off his mobile phone or 'pissed off out of it'. The lovely Fred Wedlock, compèring for John Tams and Barry Coope, was drowned out by shouts for more from the audience. He told them, 'All right—this is the awkward bit when I have to go back there and ask him if he's got a short one.' The lead singer of Bristol-based Irish band Celtic Five, David Foggarty, shocked the audience after peppering the set with more than a few Irish expletives. 'I must apologise to anyone who has young children here in the audience—you irresponsible feckin' bastards,' he said. Well, it was after the watershed! We had some great evenings at Saul over the years with the likes of Nancy Kerr and James Fagan, Last Night's Fun, Kevin Dempsey, Little Johnny England, Wild Willy Barrett, Filska, Les Barker, Oysterband, Sara Jory, Shooglenifty and last but not least, the mighty Show of Hands. We were especially lucky to arrange a rare appearance by the iconic 1970s folk-rock band Decameron with the legendary singer guitarist Johnny Coppin, and the gravel-voiced vocals of Dave Bell, who opened the set with the appropriately entitled Say Hello To The Band.

Unfortunately, the festival suffered badly from flooding just four days before the start in 2007 and had to be cancelled, a tragedy from which it never really recovered. Clive had done a sterling job and I think in the end it all got a bit too big for its own good. The final event was held in 2008, and since then I'm often asked by people with fond memories when it's going to start again but somehow, I don't think it ever will. It was fun while it lasted but ran its course.

Chapter 2

Trials and Errors

THE FIRST couple of years were spent getting used to Saul Trader on the River Severn and the Gloucester and Sharpness Canal. This taught us valuable lessons: never take anything for granted and always expect the unexpected!

A few months after the completion of the sale, we were in Gloucester Docks preparing to head off up the River Severn. I had a nucleus of mates who, like me, had a bit of time on their hands and a penchant for messing about in boats, interspersed with the odd pint or two. I still went off each year with a crowd of lads (well, I suppose to the casual onlooker, old boys would be a more appropriate term) at least once a year for a jolly on a hire boat. There were usually about six or seven of us on the trips, organised by Eddie Dunford, the landlord of almost 40 years of the Black Horse at Telham, a few miles from Battle in East Sussex. Eddie was the archetypal gentleman landlord—rosy-cheeked from the occupational hazard of his time as the cordial mine host and a smile that lit up all around him. Nobody ever heard Eddie swear and he was a fount of knowledge of all things; pubs, railways and canals being among his favourite subjects. He was like a character from some great novel, and he dismissed the chaos of life with an infectious chuckle. When you asked him what he was having to drink, he would always reply with, 'Oh—just a light ale old lad.'

Some of the jolly boys were with us on the River Severn trip. Apart from Ed, there was Mick, Paul and Malcolm. I first met Malcolm decades ago when he was the printer on the P&O liner Arcadia, and I worked in the purser's office. The drag queens on board—the life and soul of the ships in those days–referred to Malcolm as Miss Print. He'd always suffered with very bad eyesight and by now his vision had worsened to the point that he had to use a stick. He liked to get away with us and could find his way around the boat and locks. Once on the Oxford Canal he filled a lock right in the face of a boat waiting to come up. They were stroppy at first but settled down when I explained he hadn't been able to see them. Malc has since lost his sight completely. He has a beautiful Golden Retriever called Phoenix who takes him to his local, the Tudor Rose in Romsey, every afternoon for the company and the Guinness. Malcolm always came along as look-out.

Then there was Mick. Forty years at sea—most of it working for the Post Office in cable-laying ships. He was good company with loads of stories of his days in the Merchant Navy and like all good seamen, travelled light and could live for a month out of a small canvas grip. He was one of those blokes who could wear a potato sack and look like a million dollars, unlike the rest of us who could wear a million-dollar suit and still look like a sack of potatoes. He took a lot of trouble over his appearance. Mick liked the ladies—and the ladies liked Mick. His thick head of greying hair was always brushed, and his clothes were as though he'd just bought them, even though most of them were years old. He hailed from Dover and went to the boy's sea school at Chatham. He spoke with a throaty sort of slow East Kent drawl: 'Ello Dover, this is Rover, over!' When casting off Mick would shout, 'All queer fore and aft.' Paul was the cook; in real life a tyre manager for Chessington Tyres. Paul loved his food and luck-ily for us he loved cooking it too. He always brought the provisions. There'd be 17 varieties of sausage, black and white puddings… breakfast each morning was a mountainous feast, although after the first few days we were all so bloated that we reverted to muesli and toast. Paul would bring his homemade chutney and baked muffins on board, and his pièce de résistance, a potent and extremely moreish damson liquor which looked like paraffin and tasted like nectar.

On this occasion, we were moored outside the Pizza Piazza Restaurant in Gloucester Docks and it was full of office workers having lunch. Although Saul Trader has a pucker anchor on a winch, I hadn't got used to dropping it in anger. I always liked to have an anchor ready to go when I was on a river; the East Channel (or the parting, as it's called), which connects the Gloucester-Sharpness canal to the River Severn, can be a bit tricky. There's a bit of tidal flow and it's narrow and twisty, and now and again you might meet one of the grain barges that were running from Sharpness to Healing's Mill in Tewkesbury at that time. I had a spare portable anchor stowed in the forward hatch and when I went to fetch it, I found myself standing in a foot of water. The forepeak locker is separated from the rest of the boat with a watertight bulkhead. Nevertheless, there was quite a lot of gear stowed in there that shouldn't be getting wet—including the bow thruster motors.

I couldn't understand where it was coming from and after a bit of frantic head-scratching, I resorted to calling Darrell. At the time he was running the Sharpness shipyard which he'd leased from British Waterways (BW). As soon as I had explained the problem, he said, 'Hang on—I'm on my way.' Darrell was similar in stature to Ronnie Corbett—hyperactive with an excited high-pitched Derbyshire accent—and like Rupert Bear on

Benzedrine. He arrived within 20 minutes, peered into the hatch, scratched his head and, unperturbed by the crowds of gongoozlers with their mouths stuffed full of mozzarella, whipped off his shirt and trousers and stripped to his bright blue underpants—right there on the deck—and dived down below.

Five minutes later he emerged, dripping wet and shaking his head. 'It's got to be the bilge pump,' he declared. The bilge pump arrangement on Saul Trader is based on sea-going practice and it took me about six months to work it out. Simply (it's easy for me to say that now) there is one large pump that is driven continuously by a belt driven from the engine. This operates on a clutch and serves five compartment valves and a deck-wash system. The deck-wash takes in water from outside the boat, while the other side of the pump removes water from inside the boat. Only an idiot could manage to configurate the valves in such a way that water from the deck-wash could syphon back in from outside into the boat.

I was that idiot! Luckily this was discovered before starting up the river, or we could have been in big trouble. We descended the large lock that lowered us from the dock basin into the river, safely negotiated the East Channel and finally entered the River Severn proper at the parting. To the lock at Upper Lode is about ten miles. This part of the river is tidal, and the flow varies according to the heights of the tides. The Severn Estuary is famous worldwide for its tidal range, which periodically gives rise to the Severn Bore—not the bloke who sits at the end of the bar of the Red Lion at Arlingham and talks all night long about cricket, but a huge wave that sweeps up the estuary, sometimes as far as Upper Lode.

Once, we were moored with the narrowboat on the pontoon at Haw Bridge, halfway between Gloucester and Tewkesbury, and had spent a pleasant evening admiring the décor of the Bridge Inn. I was about to turn in at about midnight when suddenly all hell broke loose. The night was quiet with no wind and yet suddenly the boat started to bang and bounce around quite violently. I went out on to the well-deck thinking we were under attack and found the proverbial silent night. I was mystified. What the hell had caused this disruption? As I was about to give up and blame the beer, I saw three ducks skim by at a rate of knots. Nothing unduly significant about that except that they were going the wrong way—upstream! It then dawned on me. We had been hit by the remnants of a bore that had reversed the flow of water against the natural stream. The result was that our ropes had all switch-backed, rather like a pair of windscreen wipers, and we had been thrown around for a few minutes. No damage occurred and peace was soon restored.

The lock at Upper Lode is huge and was built to accommodate a tug and barge train. Cargoes on the Severn were at one time carried in sailing barges called trows (the 'o' in trow pronounced as in cow). One example, the Spry, was restored and displayed in the Ironbridge Gorge Museum. They were superseded in the 1940s by a small fleet of unpowered barges that could carry up to 150 tons and were hauled by tugs. They plied between Avonmouth and Stourport but were made redundant as the road networks were improved. The main problem was that, in order to reach destinations in the industrial heartlands of the Midlands, cargoes had to be transhipped at Worcester as the maximum load on the narrow canals such as the Worcester-Birmingham and the Staffs and Worcester, was just 25 tons. This was both costly and time-consuming. In the 1980s, one of these dumb barges, Sabrina 5, was restored at Saul and is displayed afloat alongside the excellent Waterways Museum in Gloucester Docks. During the Saul Canal Festival, it was given a new role as a floating theatre and decked out with a small stage and seating for 90 people. Once Bob Fox and Benny Graham appropriately performed their canal-based song and slide show called They're Coming Back To The Water, conceived by the late Jeff Dennison.

We bypassed Tewkesbury and two hours later Upton upon Severn hove into view. It is a marvellous little town on the banks of the river between Tewkesbury and Worcester. There are about ten pubs, an excellent fish and chip shop and several good restaurants all close to the water and each year they put on a series of festivals. In May it's folk, jazz in June, blues in July and over the August Bank Holiday a water festival. The latter was in full swing as we arrived; boats were tied up eight abreast, but I had made a mooring arrangement for a small consideration with Harry, who lived near the bridge on the opposite bank.

It was dusk as we motored slowly though the lines of moored boats—I felt like the First Sea Lord at the Spithead Review—and slipped quietly on to our berth in what turned out to be a prime spot. We sat on the deck and watched the floodlit procession of boats, blasting on the horn as they passed, and enjoyed a grandstand view of a fantastic firework display. The following day, we were in The Swan with a quiet lunchtime pint when a distinguished-looking gentleman, immaculately dressed in a blazer and cravat, came over to me. 'Yours the Dutchman?' he enquired. 'Fine-looking ship—damned fine.'

The next morning, we headed upstream to Worcester. Approaching the only available mooring, below the cathedral, I saw there were about 50 swans between the boat and the wall. A woman in a headscarf and two carrier bags of bread, obviously the centre of the swans' attention, was waving madly. I understand that some people feel affection towards these haughty and belligerent creatures, but why feed them with bread and encourage their greedy and intimidating behaviour? If God had wanted ducks and swans to eat bread, he'd have given them bakeries. A couple of blasts and they soon got the message, much to the disgust of the stooping tosser... of the bread, that is.

On the Worcester and Birmingham Canal, just above the first two locks, was Grist Mill Boatyard where John Luxton and Tony Stallard undertook the job of repainting the cabin and topsides, dry-docking and re-tarring the hull. Grist Mill is no longer there, although Tony has relocated to a shed nearer the river. Sadly, John passed away. He spent the last five years of his life fitting out the replica barge Isabella and never really got to use it extensively; something which had been his dream for many years.

Diglis Basin was a magical place, bustling with life and full of boats of all shapes and sizes. The lock keeper was Roger Hatchard, a former working boatman who had been at Diglis for 28 years and always had a good story to tell. He referred to his employer, BW, as 'our people'. Roger lived in the original lock keeper's cottage alongside the top lock where brass door knockers always shone like gold. Sea-going yachts nestled alongside canal cruisers in the basin, surrounded by neglected sheds, a dry dock, the wonderful Anchor Inn and Roger's immaculate cottage and office. Adjacent to the top lock was a large covered dry-dock, which had an aura about the place that's difficult to describe. You could hear the hob-nailed boots of the boatman on his way to the pub and the creaking of the pulleys as they hauled the cargoes from the holds into the warehouse lofts. On the opposite side was the magnificent façade of the Royal Worcester Porcelain Works. The company was founded in 1750 and produced fine porcelain there for more than 250 years. It's all gone now; production transferred to Stoke-on-Trent and the buildings were flattened, and BW and some developers turned it into apartments. In my opinion, Diglis was unfortunately destroyed in the name of redevelopment. Now, Roger has retired and travels on his narrow tug Lead Us. Within weeks of his departure from his job, paint began flaking from the cottage door and the brass dulled for the first time in 30 years. The end of an era.

On the return trip we decided to explore the Warwickshire Avon. There are some low bridges, and this gave us the chance to practise lowering the wheelhouse. The river was at summer level and very shallow in places. We managed to get as far as the lock at Evesham, where we stuck firmly on the bottom cill. The lock keeper offered to flush us over by opening the top paddles, but I decided it wasn't worth the hassle. I had spoken to David Bidwell from Bidworth Boats, who said it was possible to negotiate the shallows at Marcliffe with a pilot and very kindly offered his services, but it was mid–summer and very dry. The river level was falling, and I thought we could be stranded for weeks. I later learned that Darrell, some years earlier, got as far as Marcliffe and became stuck for several weeks before being rescued by the Upper Avon Navigation Trust's tug. Amazingly, in 2015, we were moored on the bank at Carcassonne on the Canal du Midi when a gentleman told us how delighted he was to see Saul Trader again. He explained he'd worked for the trust and had been in the tug gang that rescued Darrell all those years ago. We decided to turn around at Evesham. Reversing back from the lock, we hit the bottom and pushed the rudder out of its pintles. This was another valuable lesson, although I didn't exactly see it as such at the time—how to get the rudder back into place under duress.

There was a wonderful little bakery shop nearby and we lunched on freshly baked Oggies. That evening we ate in the Northwick Hotel in Waterside. The only remarkable thing about the place was the gents' loo. A tailor's dummy dressed as a hag, complete with lipstick and broomstick, sat in the corner and burst into a raucous cackle as one stood at the trough, with one's prized possession in hand! I was tempted (but discretion ultimately prevailed) to see what the ladies' cabaret had to offer!

We left Saul Trader in the lower basin at Tewkesbury Marina for a month and when we returned the river level had risen appreciably. On the exit from the marina there was an arched bridge skewed at an angle across the river. As we approached, with the current suddenly underneath the starboard quarter, I realised we were going to be swept into the side of the bridge. It was one of those point of no return moments. I probably should have put it into backwards gear, and I might have saved it—but I didn't. Instead I opted for option two, the all-or-nothing principle, so spun the wheel frantically and powered on the revs. Wrong decision—no way was Saul Trader going to straighten up. The wheelhouse roof slid along the brickwork of the arch with the sickening clatter of splintering wood. It sounded as though the wheelhouse was disintegrating. When we emerged into daylight, I ran outside to inspect the damage. I was expecting to see a crumpled pile of matchwood but to my amazement there was no visible damage. The worst occurrence was that a couple of the tongue-and-grooved planks in the roof had split, and there were some fractured glass panes, and a corner of the canvass covering was torn. Amazingly, that was it—apart, of course, from more egg on my face and a phone call to John, and we were soon back at Diglis for more work.

When the repairs were completed, Malcolm and I made our way back to Saul. On the way we moored overnight beside the Boat Inn at Ashleworth, a beautifully unspoilt tiny pub on the west bank of the river which has been in the same family since Charles II granted them a licence for liquor and exclusive ferrying rights. Real ale was served from the cask and there were sometimes as many as ten to choose from. We had a few of a local Cotswold brew, Uley Bitter. Stick to what you know, I always say! The next afternoon saw us back in the docks at Gloucester opposite the yard of Tommy Nielsen, who specialised in the restoration of wooden ships. One such was a gaff-rigged cutter with a formidable bowsprit called Svengarde. Malcolm and I were idling our time in the saloon. I was gazing out of the window when the Svengarde cast off from the opposite quay, turned through

90 degrees and came across the basin, completely out of control. It and hurtled straight into Saul Trader and, for once, I was speechless. The bowsprit rose over the top of the coach roof before rocking backwards. I thought for a moment that it was going to come straight through the window. Luckily the damage was minimal and the owner of Svengarde reluctantly apologetic. Compensation was arranged for the damage to paintwork, and John Luxton made another trip to Saul to put it right. There we left the boat at Saul again—this time for the winter.

One morning in February, I got a call from Phil Trotter at Saul Junction. 'You know Saul Trader?' he said in his inimitable Potteries drone. It was both a question and a statement. 'Yes Phil,' I replied, expecting some sort of early April Fools' joke. 'When you last saw it did it have a roof on the wheelhouse?' 'Come on Phil—it's too early in the morning.' 'Well it hasn't now!' There had been a gale during the night and apparently the wheelhouse had decided to do a Mary Poppins impression. I put the phone down and didn't know whether to laugh or cry. Half an hour later, Phil called again. John Wilkinson, bridge keeper at Parkend, a mile or so up the canal, reported that a roof had passed through his bridge at 0830 and after thinking 'that looks like Saul Trader a bit low in the water', fished it out and dragged it on to the bank. During the gale, the roof had somehow worked itself loose from its four securing toggles, taken off and flown into the air and over the top of the two large Willow Trust boats, presumably passing under the Junction footbridge and then continuing unchallenged for the two miles to Parkend.

When I went to collect it—remarkably intact, as it happened—John told how he'd once owned a Dutch barge but sold it because it was too much like hard work—heavy and tiring. At the time I thought that sounded like a bit of towpath talk. Wilky was a big, strong man and had spent most of his life on the Cut; I couldn't understand what he was talking about. Over the years however, I've gradually begun to see what it was he meant. All boats have a character (a soul, if you like) and they have a habit of reminding you from time to time who's in charge. Saul Trader certainly did: every now and then, just when I thought I'd got the hang of it and when I was least expecting it. It would behave impeccably in all sorts of difficult and potentially dangerous situations and then, as if to pull you me short, it would soon show me who was the boss.

Chapter 3

Gloucester to the Thames

A T LAST, in the spring of 2000, I found myself with enough time to head for France. There were three ways of getting there: lorry (very expensive and somewhat defeatist); Land's End (a bit precarious); or the Kennet and Avon Canal, the River Thames and the English Channel.

There was no competition really. I'd always liked the K&A since my first trip from Hilperton to Bath in a Wessex Narrowboat in 1986. At 70ft long and 13ft wide, and with a draft of 3ft 6in, Saul Trader was just about on the limit for the canal—the air draft of 7ft with the wheelhouse down might have been a problem at the notorious Newbury bridge, but that obstacle, a temporary Bailey Bridge that had been there for 50 years, had finally been raised. It was definitely worth a shot.

So, in June 2000 we motored out of Sharpness Lock on to a flat, calm Severn Estuary and headed for Bristol with not a bore in sight! I had made the trip a couple of times before with a narrowboat, and always with someone who knew the river. It could be awkward—there were rocks and whirlpools and treacherous currents underneath the bridges—but with a bit of pre-planning, a sound craft and reasonable weather conditions, the passage did not present any undue difficulties. On board with me was Scragg, Phil's heir apparent at the yard. He had been sailing in the estuary with his dad since childhood and knew it like the back of his hand. Another friend, Duncan Milne, a master mariner, came as pilot and Duncan was the sort of bloke you'd want to have with you in a 25ft yacht in a hurricane in the Bay of Biscay (not that you'd ever actually want to be in a 25ft yacht in a hurricane in the Bay of Biscay!). Duncan arrived at Sharpness with an inflatable dinghy and 25 horsepower outboard, hand-held VHF radios, a hand-held GPS, rocket flares and life jackets, and two packets of chocolate digestives.

In those days you had to sit out the tide at Avonmouth, and this entailed taking the bottom. This we did outside the entrance to the old dock at Portishead. There's a marina there now where, for about £40, you can wait in comfort and safety, and even have a few beers in the town. As a precaution we passed a rope underneath the keel. There were stories of boats sticking to the mud and not rising with the tide. I'd never actually known this happen and it was probably just an old wives' tale, but it was better to be safe, as they say. Once the boat settled, we spent the afternoon skimming across the estuary to Wales in Duncan's inflatable. We re-floated without any problems and contacted Avonmouth Radio for permission to proceed up the Avon into Bristol.

There was a huge car carrier backing into to Portishead Dock. 'Keep going across his stern,' instructed the harbour master. And I did, thankful that the skipper of the vast bulk reversing backwards towards us had also heard the message. It was an uneventful passage up the twisting River Avon, passing the small drying-out anchorage at Pill and sailing beneath the haughty Clifton Suspension Bridge, and we moored below the entrance lock into the Bristol floating harbour, once notorious as a centre of the slave trade. Once safely inside the inner harbour, we tied up opposite the Nova Scotia and went in for a much-needed pint. One of the residents of the modern dockside apartments told us how nice it was to see such a beautiful craft in the harbour and that made us feel welcome. On the way back from the pub we had a look inside the pump house containing the original hydraulic pumping system for operating the lock gates and swing bridge and were given a guided tour by the foreman.

Bristolians have a strange vernacular and a habit of adding an 'L' to words ending with 'A'. Thus, you might meet someone who drives a Ford Sierral, has just re-fitted his kitchen with Formical tops, and regards the demotion of Bristol Rovers to the fourth division as the end of an eral. From the Floating Harbour (strange name when you think about it) we slowly navigated the busy wash of the little ferries that ply to and fro, connecting Temple Meads station with landing stages at the many harbour-side attractions. The areal (sic) is surrounded with bars, museums, art galleries and shopping centres. We passed Isambard Kingdom Brunel's Great Britain, the first iron-hulled and propeller driven ocean liner, and a replical (I really must stop this now!) of The Matthew, which John Cabot sailed to North America in 1497. On through the twist and turns beneath Temple Meads Station led to the Feeder Canal and the tidal lock at Crew's Hole and the River Avon. There was a very low bridge just after the Keynsham Road that necessitated the lowering of the wheelhouse, and with the weather set fair for the next couple of days, we left it down until Saltford. Here Saul Trader was reunited briefly with its original owner, as Darrell had expanded his empire and taken over the marina.

A few weeks later we started the ascent of the Kennet and Avon Canal with Mick, Malcolm and my practical brother, Roy, who had done some jobs on the boat at Salt-ford. When we arrived at the bottom of the Widcombe flight in Bath, a couple of lads asked where we were going. 'Belgium!' I replied emphatically, 'is this the right way?' Passage through the lock flight was uneventful. At the top was a short tunnel, the Cleveland House Tunnel, and disaster struck, rudely reminding me never to make assumptions when boating. We stuck firmly at the entrance to the tunnel, and the net result was a broken rudder ram and a boiled engine. The lock keeper on the Widcombe flight was Nigel, the son of the former incumbent Jock (The Lock). Jock looked after the Widcombe locks for many years, occupying a little hut halfway up. We would often top up his cup with a tot or two of whisky, whatever the time of day. Jock would disappear with a nod into his hut and emerge minutes later with a smile and a red face and then set all the remaining locks for us. In the evenings he would be seen shovelling dirt between the gates 'to stop the leaks.' Nigel did his best to help us over the next couple of days to raise the level as much as he could, but it was hopeless. The pound between Bath Top Lock and the next lock at Bradford-on-Avon was ten miles long—that's quite a lot of water. We would have to admit defeat and go back to Saltford. This meant reversing down the flight as the canal there was much too narrow to turn around in.

Nigel suggested we waited until the evening when the steady stream of hire boats through the flight had stopped. He thought we might be able to turn below the second lock. As we reversed back to the lock, I heard the prop clanging against something hard and rocky. A kindly old lady peered over her garden wall. 'That's the bricks they chucked in when they repaired the bridge,' she said knowingly. 'I see 'em doing it.' The engine started to struggle, and I smelled hot oil, so I shut off the engine and darted below. The scene in the engine room was something like a massacre, except that instead of blood it was oil—oil and steam. I sat in the doorway and held my head in my hands. I really thought the engine had blown up. There was oil everywhere; the entire engine room was covered in the stuff.

Roy appeared and we tried to work out what had happened. Eventually, with the detached logic of a qualified toolmaker, Roy got the answer and it wasn't as bad as we'd first thought. A pinched coolant hose (probably damaged when we'd struggled to get free of the rocks at the entrance to the tunnel a couple of days before), had caused the engine to overheat. This had boiled the water in the calorifier tank which at the time was venting via the pressure relief valve into the engine bilge (we later changed it). This, in turn, raised the level to such an extent that the bilge pump pulley had become submerged and it was spraying hot oil and boiling water all around the engine room. In the event, it cost £8 for a length of hose and about four hours cleaning up the mess. By the time we had finished it was 2.30am. We had a large glass of Laughing Frog and turned in, knackered.

The next morning, we reversed ignominiously down the top three locks before being able to turn and run away back down the river to Saltford to the amusement of some of the locals, and gave some unexpected business to Bath Narrowboats, who did an excellent job on the rudder. Luckily the lads I had cockily asked about Belgium were nowhere to be seen. Nigel suggested we try again the following year as the lining work and bank reinforcement would then be complete, enabling the weir level to be raised on the pound to Bradford-on-Avon, providing an extra 180mm of water (five or six inches to you and me, or three to the proverbial Welsh wife!) And so, after wintering at Saltford and sitting out floods and foot-and-mouth disease, we were at last ready for another go. As usual there was no shortage of friendly advice.

'You'll never get through Bradford.'
'You're too big to get around the bend on to Avon-
cliffe Aqueduct.'
'I got stuck at Hilperton and I only draw 2ft.'
'You're never going to get through the Semington
swing bridge—you're too wide.'

There were one or two comments that did worry me a little. Lots of people warned me of the dog-leg bridge at Martinslade, just before Devizes. And Graham (Shag) Lee—15 years at Wessex Narrowboats—said we might have a problem at Lock 37 on the Caen Hill flight as it was narrower than the rest and couldn't take a breasted pair of narrowboats. As in all these cases, if you listen to enough advice, you'll eventually hear the piece you want. Bill Fisher, whose opinion I respected, told me what I really wanted to hear. 'You'll get through OK,' he said. I also spoke to Adrian Stott, who had done the passage of the canal in his Dutch Tjalk, slightly smaller than Saul Trader, a few years earlier and told me to 'go for it—we need boats like yours to prove it's possible and to make sure BW lives up to its promises.' That was it then—we were going for it.

The timing was perfect. There was plenty of water after the wettest winter in centuries, the bulk of the work on the canal had been completed (or so I thought) and the forecast was for reasonably dry and settled weather (essential as the wheelhouse would have to be down most of the time). So, on the afternoon of April 11th we backed out of Saltford Marina, hopefully for the last time, and with a blast on the horn headed for Bath. Then it started to rain. There was only one low bridge between Saltford and Bath. For some inexplicable reason the pedestrian Churchill footbridge had a headroom of about 8ft at normal river levels. Rather than dismantle the roof in the rain we decided to moor for the night on the towpath before the bridge and in fact found it a convenient place for access to the centre of Bath. Another Bristolian I knew said they called it Bawth; that on Friday nights they had a baaaf and Saturday mornings went shopping in Bawth.

An early start the following morning with the weather bright and clear saw us successfully through the deepest lock on the English canal system at 19.5ft to the top of the Widcombe flight without incident by noon, where we tied up right against the side—still afloat—for lunch. This was a tremendous improvement on the first attempt and proof that the level had indeed been raised, or at least that the bottom was now a little bit further from the top! The canal here was some 65ft above the River Avon. Far below the Great Western main line to Bristol ran through Sydney Gardens, where spotters and photographers would stand to watch the Kings and Castles striding through with their Paddington expresses. Now, a future icon, British Rail's High-Speed Train, had taken over passenger duties.

I was almost lulled into a false sense of belief that the next 75 miles to Reading would be just as easy, but that theory was very soon shattered—after just 100 yards to be precise, as we grounded once again under the Sydney Wharf Bridge. With a little coaxing Saul Trader bumped and scraped through and gently edged towards Cleveland House Tunnel. I had been worried about being stuck inside the tunnel, particularly after the last episode, with narrowboats full of hurried holidaymakers queueing and cursing at each end. As it was, after another couple of shunts, a few more revs than were really good for it and a lot of smoke, we were through and out into the daylight. Then we crawled over the bottom to Bathampton, the two miles taking four hours. Although most people we met, boaters and towpath walkers, were welcoming and supportive, and glad to see us having a go, some were less enamoured by our presence. One resident boater at Bathampton complained that our speed had loosened one of his mooring pins! At half-a-mile an hour it was difficult to go much slower and steer, and with a displacement weight of some 60 tons, impossible to safeguard mooring pins driven into soft mud.

A good meal in the George at Bathampton put us in better spirits for the next stage. I wanted to get to Bradford-on-Avon by the evening but that proved over-optimistic. The going was extremely slow, but we were making progress. By lunchtime we had reached Dundas—almost. Just before the aqueduct, underneath the horse-bridge, we went hard aground. Contractors had been working on the channel and were still clearing the site. Finally, after an hour of thinking about it, the gang managed to bow-haul us over the obstacle. Apparently, a temporary concrete cill had not been removed, restricting the normal depth. As we floated towards the turn for the aqueduct, I suddenly realised I had no steering. On inspection we found that the rudder had been dislodged by the movement over the concrete and was fouling the stock bracket. This was quickly fixed by Scragg, luckily for him without the need for any sub-aqua activity—it was still only April. It was Good Friday (the 13th as it happened) and the gang was naturally eager to get home to Wales for the weekend. Little did we realise then as we waved goodbye, we would be seeing some of them again very soon.

Passage across the Dundas Aqueduct went remarkably well, and it wasn't until almost 5pm when we came to another sudden and grinding halt just past the bridge at Limpley Stoke. This was different, and I knew immediately that this, whatever it was, was not going to yield to any amount of shunting or bow-hauling. This was an immovable object and we were an irresistible force. Good Friday at 5pm—not the best time to get assistance. Luckily Nigel, son of Jock, had given me his mobile number. It was the first day of his holiday and he was in the pub. His team, Leeds United, had just beaten Liverpool (blimey, it must have been a long time ago!) and he was enjoying it. In fact, he was as overjoyed as a newt! But fair play to him, he contacted the duty men and an hour later Kevin Osborne and his mate Ray arrived in an Astra van. Surely, they weren't going to try to tow us out with that. Kevin got out and walked towards us, shaking his head. I thought he was going to say, 'that bloody boat's too big for this canal.' Instead, to my relief, he said, 'I knew it. I bloody knew it. They haven't cleared the bloody rubble.' 'They' were the Welshmen we'd met earlier and that was how we came to meet them again. Their weekend break was about to be rudely interrupted. In the course of lining the section over the winter, they'd built a concrete ramp from the towpath to access their equipment and broke it up when they'd finished the job, leaving the broken bits in the cut, as you do! 'Are you sure they were Welsh and not Irish?' asked Scragg. This was what formed the immovable object and rather buggered up their Easter hols! BW then swung into action with a rare commitment; the sort of reaction you get from people who are thankful that, for a change, that particular problem was not actually their fault. I got regular calls throughout the evening from Kevin and the BW project engineer, keeping us informed of progress.

The contractors were summoned from their weekend off and would return in the morning with a rubber duck, an excavator on rubber tyres, to clear it out. The only sensible thing in the circumstances was to wander down the lane to the wonderful Hop Pole in the village of Limpley Stoke for a couple of pints of Guinness, the problem, for the time being at least, resolved. There were far worse places to be stranded. The 16th century Hop Pole, all beams and log fires and excellent draft bitter, also served a very agreeable steak and ale pie. Limpley Stoke lies in the valley of the River Avon, at the bottom of the hill from the canal. Scragg, in his inimitable style, suggested that the name conjured images of lazy sex! The railway station is on the main Salisbury-Bristol line and enjoyed 15 minutes of fame as the setting for the Ealing comedy The Titfield Thunderbolt.

The promise of the contractors returning in the morning actually materialised as the afternoon. At 2pm two men returned from Carmarthen, fetched the rubber duck from Bradford and removed about three tons of what looked like extremely good quality hard concrete lumps and rocks from the bed of the canal. Eventually I got the signal to try again—and again came to a grinding halt. After several repeats as the pile of recovered rocks grew higher and higher, we had to resort to a drag from the hydraulic arm of the digger and slowly bumped over the last few remaining boulders. I tried not to listen to the squeals of protest from Saul Trader's bottom, putting my trust in the quality of the steel used by RW Davis & Son. We were over that particular obstacle—bring on the next.

The rest of the day was relatively easy, going slow over the bottom as far as Avoncliffe and without any of the problems forecast by the prophets of doom, we sailed sweetly over the aqueduct and into... deep water! At least it felt deep. For the first time in days we were actually cruising, on about 1,000 revs, and into Bradford-on-Avon by teatime. What a difference a bit of dredging and a new lining can make. We were so pleased with ourselves, and I really did start to think (quite wrongly, as it turned out) that we'd cracked it. We had a convivial evening in the Canal Tavern with my old mate Graham Lee. Graham, known to everyone as Shag or The Vulgar Boatman, started the first hire fleet on the K&A in 1985 at Hilperton. We reminisced about those times. I hired one of his boats in 1986 when I first discovered the wonderful market town of Bradford-on-Avon, home to a once thriving woollen industry. Bradford had some 30 working mills which flourished until the early 19th century. At that time Bradford was the headquarters of the Avon Rubber Company and Moulton Cycles. The Avon is crossed by way of a Norman bridge complete with its own little gaol, and alongside the canal stands a 180ft long listed Tithe Barn. Then there is the Canal Tavern, alongside which we were moored. In those days it was run by Pete and Judy.

Pete sported one of those droopy moustaches that made him look gloomier than he was. Above the bar there was a photograph of him standing beside a plastic boat and wearing a red and white Ferrari cap and matching anorak. Someone had written underneath 'Would you buy a used boat from this man?' One morning he appeared on the towpath looking even more miserable than usual. We were about to cast off and I said, 'Come on Pete, jump on and come for a ride.' 'I'd like to,' he replied sadly, 'but it would be injurious to me health. I.e. 'er indoors would kill me.'

In those days, the lock at Bradford-on-Avon was kept locked and you could only go through under the supervision of the lock keeper. Mick Mold was in charge of the section then and a more amiable helpful and dedicated bloke you couldn't wish to meet. Eventually they put in a computerised back pumping system at a cost, so rumour had it, of £85,000. I was moored outside the Canal Tavern once with Eddie when Mick Mold came over and asked if he could borrow the boat's shaft and had we got a plastic lemonade-type bottle and a nail. 'It's the bloody pump control again,' he explained. We were intrigued—what could you possibly do with a pole and a lemonade bottle that was not illegal? 'We need to nail the bottle to a pole and shove it up the inlet to try to kick the bloody computer into life," said Mick, managing to keep a straight face. The cutting edge of modern technology!

How Eddie chuckled. It reminded me of an old joke the cricket commentator Brian Johnston used to delight in telling. A honeymoon couple on a tandem holiday get to a hill. Two old ladies are sitting on the grass having a picnic when he says, 'We'll get off here—you get down and I'll push it up.' One of the ladies passed out and her friend choked on her cream puff!

On another occasion we needed to lock through after working hours. 'No problem,' said Mick, 'just say a time and I'll be here.' 'But surely you don't want to come all the way from Devizes just for us," I said, "can't you get Wally to do it?' Wally was his long-haired and silent assistant, and I knew he lived locally in Bradford. 'Wally!' said Mick, tossing back his head. 'You must be joking—we wouldn't let him anywhere near a bloody lock.' Sadly, Mick is no longer with us; they say the good die young.

We woke the next morning with sore heads. The next two miles to Hilperton took us the whole day. Nothing insurmountable like concrete, just mud—two feet thick. The progress was painful. I had to stop the engine a dozen times to clear the mud filter and at one point we gave up, switched off and watched some of the Grand Prix on the TV. We didn't need to tie up; we were moored on mud. I topped up with 100 gallons of diesel at Bradford Marina and was told later that the section hadn't been dredged for ten years; at Biss Aqueduct we had to squeeze past a rusting bright green dredger. A boater laughed that the dredger itself had stuck there and the driver told him it was worse than the place he'd actually been dredging! The bridge holes, as usual, were the worst and I thought we would never get through the one just before the marina at Hilperton.

We only made a few more yards before the next impasse at Hilperton Road Bridge where we stayed, about 4ft from the bank, for the night. The level looked to me to be about 3in or 4in down and so once again I had to call on the good offices of Kevin Osborne. He explained another miracle of modern science. 'All I have to do is punch in a code on my mobile phone and the computer on the pumps at Bradford will send a message back stating the level above and below the lock and which of the pumps is activated—brilliant isn't it? Mind you it's usually wrong!' They'd obviously not yet discovered Mick Mold's barge pole and lemonade bottle technique! And it certainly was wrong, as a visual inspection at Bradford proved. A good old-fashioned manual override was called for, and an hour later we had enough water to gently slide through the bridge and continue our crawl eastwards. It was now Easter Monday, a beautiful sunny day, but I think I spent more time down below clearing the mud filter than I did enjoying the sunshine. The constant strain on the engine pushing through unrelenting silt took its toll and between the two Whaddon bridges and resulted in the impeller on the raw water intake finally giving up the ghost. We were stuck fast in the middle of the cut with the engine disabled, with five narrowboats and a wide-beam cruiser behind and three more coming the other way.

The result—unhappiness and frustration! Everybody mucked in to help. Some people walking the towpath joined in on the head rope to pull us as far as possible out of the middle of the channel. There was another irony here: the boat that we were wedged against, Arthur, belonged to me. It was in a sponsored boat agreement with Wessex Narrowboats! By chance we found that the bilge pump had the same type of impeller and while I bow-hauled all the narrowboats past, Craig (aka Scragg; I always called him by his proper name when there was work to be done) cannibalised the pump and replaced the knackered impeller—two blades left out of 12! After about half an hour we were on the move again—slowly. I had called Barry Sims, of Wilts Marine Services, who responded brilliantly and appeared as if by magic on the towpath 20 minutes later with a replacement impeller. That's service for you on a Bank Holiday.

Semington Swing Bridge, although wide enough despite the advice I received, proved exceptionally obstinate and meant we had to resort to using the Tirfor winch for the first time. This is an ingenious piece of kit which facilitates moving very heavy loads by means of elaborate gearing. Basically, you connect one end to something solid like a tree or a bollard. The steel wire cable passes through the machine and the other end is secured to the object you need to move, and then with a bit of grunt and heave you pull a lever attached to the thing backwards and forwards and, hopefully, the immovable object slowly moves. If you get the impression that I really had no idea how the Tirfor works, then you're not far out.

We finally inched our way through, although at one point there was a good 8in of hull showing out of the water. We got to the bottom of Semington at 7.30pm as dusk fell, and Malcolm went ahead to set the lock. His eyesight was gradually getting worse. He suffered from a form of the degenerating disease known as retina pigmentosa and was by this time officially registered as blind. Even so, he still refused to use a stick. As he started to raise the bottom paddle to empty the lock, someone came out of the cottage and started off about not being allowed to work locks after dark. Malc didn't look up. 'Is it dark?' he said innocently, 'I wouldn't know mate, I'm a blind man.'

At 8pm we tied up in the pound between the locks. Had we now finally broken the back of it? I wasn't really surprised that the answer was an emphatic no. I stayed on the boat for a couple of days at Semington while the crew went home. I would have liked to have got the boat into the dry dock there for a cursory check of the prop and the state of the bottom but unfortunately this wasn't possible as Saul Trader's draft was too deep to clear the cill. Nevertheless, I had a good clear-up and got the place shipshape, and by the end of the week we were ready to go again.

Above Semington progress was disappointingly slow but by lunchtime the bottom lock at Seend appeared on the horizon. There were contractors working here too on the towpath—another lot this time—and after having the first lock literally stolen in front of my eyes by a dubious looking character on an even more dubious looking boat, we climbed the first four locks without any problems. Then a messenger came running down from the top lock with information from the contractor, Greenford. 'We heard that you were on the way, but we didn't expect you quite so soon.' That was a bit strange as we had only been making about 400 yards an hour. Apparently one of the bottom gates would not open enough to pass our width and a diver had been summoned from Reading to investigate. They were full of apologies and 'please bear with us we'll get you through as soon as we can'. I soon discovered why they were so attentive as I watched the diver fill at least a dozen buckets with rubble (contractor's rubble) that had been blocking the gate. They told me that it had been thrown in 'by the kids.'

From there to Foxhangers was suddenly much better—the engine was not labouring anymore and there was no smoke, and we were doing a comfortable two knots. We were boating again at long last after a week of driving along the bottom. In the evening I spoke to someone on a narrowboat who told me that he had called BW to warn of our approach and instigated the visit of the diver to Seend. It was very considerate and saved us a lot of time. I wonder how long it would have been left had we not needed the full width of the lock. We ate that night in the Three Magpies at Rowde and set ourselves up nicely for the ascent of the Caen Hill flight of locks—all 27 of them virtually one after the other, raising the canal by 237ft.

At Limpley Stoke, I'd met Robert Coles, a well-known railway and canal photographer, connoisseur and champion of the cause, who had asked me to let him know when we reached Foxhangers so he could take pictures. I'd also arranged for Trevor and Verity Appleby, friends from Shaftesbury, to come over for the day and so it was doubly embarrassing that at the bottom of the 'straight sixteen', the engine started to falter and eventually stopped altogether. It had been spluttering since we started up from Foxhangers and was obviously suffering from a lack of fuel. I dived below and changed the filters and checked the fuel level, all to no avail.

Trevor, who knows about these things, decided it was a problem with the hand priming pump and set about dismantling it. The lock-wheeling party and Robert and his wife Pat looked on patiently as we worked on the pump. I was dreading a split diaphragm or some such thing that we would have difficulty in replacing at midday on a Saturday, but thankfully it was just a blocked gauze filter which simply required a good clean. I thought nothing of it at the time but over the next few years it was to become a source of constant trouble. By 1.30pm we were ready to tackle the flight. Everyone worked marvellously as a team and two hours later we were at the Black Horse at the top of the climb. At one point I said to Trevor, 'must be Lock 37 next.' 'No,' he said, 'that was the last one.' So once again our fears were unfounded, and we had passed through the narrowest lock of the flight without even realising it. By 5pm we were tied opposite the Devizes Wharf and Robert took more photographs of the crew while we had a cup of tea and a round of choc ices. Once more I found myself asking the question, 'are we now over the worst?' And once more the unspoken answer was a resounding no!

So far, we had been incredibly lucky with the weather. Apart from the first day when it rained on the way to Bath, it stayed fine. Each day we took down the wheelhouse in the morning and was able to leave it down. Although we could have squeezed under some of the bridges with it in situ, it would have been a very tight fit and really not worth the risk of causing damage again. On the Sunday morning at Devizes, however, all that changed, and what started as a fine drizzle gradually got worse. By the time we reached Pewsey Wharf everything and everybody was thoroughly soaked to the skin. The sad thing was this was some of the finest landscape of the whole canal—the Vale of Pewsey and the White Horse carved in chalk in the hillside… this was Crop Circle country.

A pub called The Barge at Honeystreet was where Fred Wedlock, another personality I knew from the Saul

Festival, often played. Fred had a wickedly funny sense of humour. I had the pleasure of sitting with him at breakfast during one of the Cromer folk festivals when he almost gave me indigestion from laughing so much at his stories. He had a shock of curly hair and a permanent smile that lit up concert halls. Sometimes he was a bit near the mark and would get into trouble at times, performing for the like of the WI. Once at a gig in a pub he said he had been asked for a request. 'Cor blimey,' he told the audience, 'I haven't sung that song for must be 20 year. I recorded it a long time ago on a 7-inch. That's how long ago that was. Cor—who remembers the 7-inch? What I'd give for that now eh—seven inches. Better'n this bloody great thing they've given me!' Fred passed away in 2010, a lovely man sadly missed.

For the first time since leaving the Avon at Bath, we had had plenty of water underneath us. Throughout the whole of the long pound through Bishops Canning and Honey Street we swam effortlessly and but for the atrocious weather would have enjoyed a fine day's cruising. I'd been looking forward to reaching Pewsey Wharf. Graham (Shag) Lee had just moved into a cottage with a view to opening up the old wharf building as The Waterfront Cafe. He was as excited as I was about the arrival of Saul Trader and as we passed through Bridge 114, I gave a couple of long and loud blasts on the horn to announce our arrival. I expected him to come rushing out waving flags and blowing trumpets, but there was no sign of him.

He'd fallen asleep in front of the fire and hadn't heard us coming! What a bloke!

We were there, at Pewsey, almost halfway to Reading. Surely, I could say we'd broken the back of it… couldn't I? We left the boat at Pewsey Wharf for a week to catch up on some work at home, and Graham did not waste the opportunity of some free publicity for his new venture. The Wiltshire Gazette published a nice little article complete with a large photograph of Graham standing proudly beside the boat under the banner headline GIANT BARGE MAKES WAVES. Well I certainly hoped it hadn't—difficult in two foot of silt at half-a-mile an hour! Graham had always been one for a bit of self-promotion. He had sold the hire company at Hilperton, Wessex Narrowboats, a couple of years previously, and had taken a lease from BW on the wharf at Pewsey. He appeared in several TV shows on the canal made with Timothy West and Prunella Scales. On one occasion the prop shaft on their narrowboat had broken and Prunella said, 'There was only one thing for it. We had to call on our knight in shining blue overall', and up stepped Graham, a toolbox in each hand. After lifting the engine cover, he apparently exclaimed, 'Fucking 'ell what a mess!' and the director raised his arms in the air. 'Cut, cut! Oooh this is a family show you know, take two, and Graham—language please, darling!'

Some years later, The Waterways Recovery Group (or Wergies as they are known) a band of volunteers who do sterling work clearing and restoring canals, invited me to the opening of Over Basin at the Gloucester end of the Hereford Canal. It was being officially opened by none other than Mr West and Miss Scales. When Graham heard this 'free publicity' immediately flashed before his eyes. 'Tell Pru that Shag has opened a café at Pewsey Wharf,' he said. 'Surely she won't know you as Shag,' I replied. 'Of course she will,' he insisted, 'make sure you tell her.' Against my better judgement I managed to get behind Miss Scales in the queue for the buffet. 'I have a message for you,' I whispered. 'Shag says to tell you he's opened a café at Pewsey Wharf.' The first thing that became immediately apparent is that Prunella Scales is definitely *not* like Sybil Fawlty. She bawled across the marquee to Mr West in a shrill tone that was more RSC than Fawlty Towers. 'Darling—do we know Shag?' 'What, a boat called Shag?' Darling bellowed back, as I prayed for the ground to open up beneath me. Shag, you owe me a pint—or six!

Next, we headed East again for Wootton Rivers and the summit pound. The K&A is almost perfectly symmetrical between Bath and Reading with Burbage Wharf on the summit pound. Exactly halfway from Bath to the summit there are 48 uphill locks to Wootton Rivers Top, followed by a four-mile pound and the 500-yard Bruce Tunnel before Crofton Top Lock and then 52 downhill locks to County Lock at Reading. I knew the summit had been dredged because I had watched them doing it;

ex-working boatman Ted Shaw was in charge of the job and I knew there was a depth of at least 4ft. What I hadn't realised but soon found out was they hadn't dredged the tunnel.

Bruce Tunnel carries the canal under the main Great Western Railway line through the Savernake Forest. It is only 500 yards long and just wide enough for one wide-beam boat. Scragg went ahead to make sure nobody entered from the opposite direction and with a long blast on the horn, we plunged into the darkness. Well, pottered, to be more accurate. It took 45 fume-choked minutes to get through, the boat scraping painfully from one side wall to the other at will, without any means of steerage. I was very happy when we eventually crept out into the sunshine. Crofton Locks mark the start of the descent to the Thames and we negotiated the flight without undue problems, accompanied by hoots and waves from the drivers of the First Great Western high-speed trains as they sped past. It was a sobering thought that they would be in Bath in about 30 minutes on a journey that had taken us nearly a month!

At Crofton there is a restored steam-powered beam engine which was originally used to pump the four miles from the reservoir at Wilton Water to the summit. It can be seen working on high days and holidays throughout the year. When we passed all was quiet, the chimney solemnly overlooking proceedings. The depth of water in the pounds varied considerably. Some had ample depth and others barely passable with the loss of steerage, resulting in Saul Trader attempting to enter the next lock sideways. It was dark and starting to spit with rain as we approached Great Bedwyn (Girt Bidden to the locals) and I decided to get the wheelhouse up before we soaked everything again. There was a narrowboat conveniently tied just at the end of the wharf and so we gratefully accepted their offer to breast up for the night. We ate in the Three Tuns (an excellent meal) accompanied by an unexpected free pint courtesy of Shag, who had organised it with the landlord, and we were (unusually) too tired to stay on for a second.

The next morning dawned with pouring rain and blowing a gale and I decided to sit tight. It would have been almost impossible to control the boat in the wind and highly unpleasant with the roof down, so we took the opportunity to catch up with some routine jobs around the boat. Luckily the next morning was brighter and more settled, and so were underway by 7am. We stopped below the lovely Little Bedwyn lock for breakfast and headed slowly and ponderously east towards Froxfield.

At Cobblers Lock there is a nice little cottage; I think children's TV presenter Johnny Morris once lived there. The present owner kept a large variety of rare and odd-looking chickens, all doing Johnny Morris impersonations! After emptying the lock, we realised the footbridge across the tail was very low. We had to take off parts of the anchor winch and deflate the Avon dinghy which was stowed on the aft roof so we could get under. We finally managed to squeeze out. On the wall at the exit from the lock, the chickens had lined up to see what all the fuss was about and stood there roaring with raucous laughter over our plight. Cobblers to you too, mate!

This is followed by another lock on Hungerford Common with a heavy swing footbridge across it, which needed to be opened while using the lock. After another brief stop for a rain shower we reached Hungerford by mid-afternoon, where we stocked up on a few provisions. We decided to press on during the afternoon and tied up at Kintbury alongside the railway line at teatime. One of the nice things about doing the K&A this way was that it gave us so much more time to take things in. I had been through here with the narrowboat several times in the past but from the wheelhouse of a Dutch barge the vista is totally different, and with the speed we were doing, there was plenty of time to enjoy it. I'd never stopped at Kintbury before, but the village was an absolute delight. River, railway and canal combine, a sylvan weir stream flowing steadily beneath the road beside the level crossing, a pathway through the 13th century churchyard to a row of typical village shops with a queue outside the bakers, the smell of fresh bread in the air, at 7.30am, and the busy, friendly and ambient Dundas Arms, serving good food and Guinness. What more could a man desire? 'It's real noice,' said Scragg. 'Yes—quite sylvan,' I agreed. 'What's that mean then?' he asked. 'I suppose it's forest-like, idyllic, lush, verdant, green.' 'Ah—like noice then.'

The level crossing was permanently manned as the line was busy day and night with freight as well as high-speed passenger trains. The friendly signalman told me a steam-hauled special was expected so we stayed to watch it. A Great Western Castle class, No 5029 Nunney Castle rushed by in a blur of Brunswick green and brass and steam, with 12 chocolate-and-cream coloured coaches in tow, the driver leaning out of his cab to wave to the signalman. It could have been 1960 but for the queue of modern cars taken by surprise at this sudden explosion from the glorious past of the Great Western Railway. And then it was gone. With a clang of the gate warning device and the whirr of the automatic barriers, we were back in the modern day; the next train a ubiquitous and boring DMU. There was time for a nostalgic sigh before starting the engine and heading off toward Newbury.

Now there was another factor to take into account (and one that was to become increasingly significant)—a following current on the River Kennet. This was great at first as we motored effortlessly along at a very smart pace. Now and again the stern would be caught in the flow and swept sideways, sending the bow in to the bank, or worse, the trees. It took careful concentration to keep the boat straight, but it was easy to be caught unaware. With a barge, the reaction of the bow to the turns of the wheel is a delicate balance. Once you lose it and get off course, it is all too easy to over-react on the opposite helm until the over-correction accelerates to the point where the bow is weaving crazily from side to side and you start to write your name in the wake! It then takes a bit of skill and experience to slow the movement down and bring the boat back to a steady course without stemming the bow into the bank.

At last the 16th century church of St Nicholas at Newbury came into view as we approached the West Mills swing bridge. I remembered it from narrowboat days as being a bit awkward—myself older but unfortunately not wiser. There was a deceptive amount of flow behind us and I decided to tie up before the bridge while we opened it. There was a line of moored narrowboats on the towpath side which made it difficult to get alongside, but that wasn't really any excuse. We failed to get a line ashore from the stern quickly enough and were pushed across in the current until the port quarter came to rest gently against a large oak tree. We had managed to get a bow line ashore, but the back end was firmly stuck, and we were jammed across the cut. No amount of reverse or heaving on the line would shift us. Some volunteer locals helped on the end of a line from the stern and eventually we were pulled free of the tree and bumped semi-sideways through the ridiculously tiny opening in the bridge. Here the channel widens appreciably, and we were able to tie up on the West Mills wharf, catch our breath and contemplate the next move. Then I noticed that the wheelhouse door would not open properly. The rail on the port side had been bent inwards to the extent that it now rubbed the outside of the door. The contact with the tree had pushed it inwards some 45 degrees! Not the end of the world but just another little job to add to the list.

I had a look at the narrow channel through the town and the notorious temporary bridge that, before its recent raising, had been the lowest on the K&A. I measured the clearance at roughly at 8ft, luxury indeed. If this at least wouldn't pose any problem, the raging torrent through the narrows certainly would. It swirled and bubbled like a witch's cauldron through the ornamental stone arched Newbury Bridge. I didn't like the look of it at all and back at the boat I telephoned Bill Fisher to ask his advice. Bill had been on the canal in Newbury for almost 40 years and knew it as well as anyone. He said he'd taken a pair of hotel narrowboats, Snipe and Taurus, down through the lock on the previous day—backwards. Logically it made good sense as that way the bow would be facing into the current and the boat's speed could be controlled with the engine and bow thrusters. He said I would be able to wind (that's canal speak for 'turn around') at West Mills above the lock and again at Newbury Wharf. For the first time since leaving Saltford I was feeling a bit apprehensive.

The winding itself was no problem. The lock was set and the gates open, and I gently eased the boat backwards towards it. There was quite a strong cross current pulling towards the weir on my port-side and as I started to correct the movement, I suddenly realised I had no bow thrusters. Of all the times for these to decide to pack up! After several forward bursts on the prop and frenzied spinning of the wheel I managed to get Saul Trader backwards into the lock. We'd had a couple of problems starting the engine during the day and I hadn't connected this at the time, but it now dawned on me that these same batteries also powered the thrusters. It crossed my mind to abort but at that moment the bottom gates opened. I couldn't go back now. There was no point in putting off the evil moment.

At the same time, I noticed crowds of early evening drinkers in the Lock Stock and Barrel on the terrace right alongside the arched bridge, probably hoping for a grandstand view of impending disaster. I eased the throttle and moved slowly backwards into the stream, and the crew jumped back on board. BW had had the sense to put flotation fenders along each side of the arch, which left just about enough room for us to pass between them. Going backwards I had almost total control of the boat, after more wrestling with the wheel as the cross current from the weir stream attempted to sweep us into the bridge parapet. I lined the boat centrally and gradually inched through the arch, with the crew fending off as best they could. At the other side of the bridge the river widened slightly and bent first one way and then the other before reaching the temporary bridge. Here the water raced and swirled furiously in a confused lumping mass that could have hosted an Olympic kayak slalom race. Without bow thrusters it was increasingly difficult to keep the bow in the centre of the channel. Eventually the current won, and we were swept out of control into the far wall. We clumped and buffeted by another pub, The Hobgoblin, which was also full of drinking spectators enjoying the unexpected cabaret. No number of forward revs seemed to have any effect on straightening us up and we nudged slowly along the wall. For one moment I thought the high stem post of Saul Trader was going to smash through a window of the pub but thankfully we bounced clear.

Eventually I was able to get some control over the bow and steer it into the current and away from the wall. The flow seemed to dissipate slightly as we neared the temporary bridge. After a couple more manoeuvres Saul Trader was lined up perfectly for the outer channel of the notorious bridge and we passed below with a good 18in to spare. In the process we managed to brush the channel direction arrow sign and turn it 180 degrees, so it pointed to the wrong side of the opening! As we made fast to Newbury Town Wharf, I breathed a sigh of relief and thought how much more difficult the last few minutes would have been had the temporary bridge not been raised; it had previously been about 7ft. I don't think I would have attempted it at all.

The following morning, we winded at the wharf. Bill had recommended turning with the stern to the north bank, which we did, and with about 3ft of the counter overhanging the footpath and 6in to spare at the front, we fairly flew around as the current got hold of the beam, coming to rest gently alongside. We were now facing the right way. The new bridge carrying the A34 across the river was very wide but because the sides of the arch sloped downwards at the edges, I decided to motor through with someone on a line ashore at both ends to ensure the flow didn't take over and push us into the edge again. What I hadn't allowed for was the pull of the weir on the far side of the bridge, which sucked us sideways and superglued us to the protective barrier. We were there for two hours before finally managing to extricate ourselves from this last Newbury hazard, with judicious use of the Tirfor and some willing local labour on the end of the shaft.

We tied for the night just above Greenham Lock, adjacent to Bill's immaculate boatyard where his wife Sue had told us there would probably be enough depth, and I decided to stay there until we had had a chance to sort out the bow thrusters. Not a record for distance travelled in a day—just about 500 yards, I suppose—but one small section I was glad to have put behind us. We still had some narrow fast-flowing bits ahead—Woolhampton and Reading, for example, which I knew were going to be a challenge to say the least, unless the flow subsided substantially. It didn't: there was so much water on the Wiltshire Plain that had nowhere to go, apart from, it seemed, into the River Kennet. Bill Fisher came and gave some very good advice. He felt that Woolhampton was passable with care and explained the best way to tackle it. When I mentioned getting stuck on the weir, he said I should've asked BW to lower the paddle gear and stop the flow while we extricated ourselves. Why didn't I think of that?

Finally, 44 days after starting out from Saltford, I made the decision to tackle the final leg to the River Thames. For all the water that had been giving us so much problems over the past few weeks, we soon discovered there wasn't enough of it in the cut. The bottom was most definitely too near the top once again. After just two miles from Greenham Lock, we had to call out BW to get us off the mud. This time it was Nick who gave up a Sunday evening to come out to Long Cut where we had come to a grinding halt halfway between Widmead and Monkey Marsh Locks. Nick got us moving by backing up the level but by the time we reached Midgham, it was getting dark so we moored on the lock bollards where we could get reasonably close to the side.

The next morning, we made an early start and arrived at the lock at Woolhampton by about 8am. If we were to make an almighty cock-up, at least we wouldn't be doing it in front of hundreds of spectators. The problem is that at the bottom of the lock the Kennet re-entered at right angles, causing a cross current, followed very closely by an electrically operated swing bridge with a very narrow gap at an angle to the left. Undeterred, we followed Bill's advice and gently motored out of the lock, having first set the bridge and with a long line walked from the stern to check the weigh should the need arise. In the event, the exercise was carried out to perfection. The force of the stream pushed us to the left at first but then the bow swung back to starboard, I threw the wheel over and suddenly we were aligned exactly for the bridge. The only way, I had been told, was to power through and hope for the best. More by luck than judgement, we shot through the narrow gap hardly touching the side. A hotel boat skipper who was watching on told me he'd never seen it done better! The stern rope was turned around a bollard on the far side of the bridge and Saul Trader swung gently alongside the landing stage, as if asking what all the fuss had been about. Now I really did think we were getting there. Just Reading and we would be on the mighty Thames. On through Aldermaston (no problem) and Padworth Locks (OK but for a bit of bumping on hard lumpy things in the lock channel). We were sailing, and then…

I had left the boat at Towney Lock with Scragg in charge to set the swing bridge at Ufton and sat in the sunshine to wait for the boat. And waited. And waited. Until it became obvious there was no boat. I wandered back towards the lock and there it was, firmly stuck again with about a foot of the hull out of the water, just a couple of boat lengths from the lock itself. There was no alternative than to call on BW in the shape of Nick once again, who came with Tirfor and man. After about an hour of sweat and toil, we were dragged over another bank of sticky toffee pudding. All optimism had deserted us, so at least we were not disappointed to go aground again at Tyle Mill (where Nick backed up the level). But even so we were not prepared for Garston, where at 5pm and with thoughts of thirst-quenching Guinness on our lips, we grounded at the confluence of the river stream. Where the lock cut re-entered the river on a bend, a huge bank of silt had built up—and we were comfortably sat upon it. This time we were stuck like glue. I had got to know instinctively when we ground to a halt whether there was any chance of wriggling off again and this was not one of them. Out came our old friend Nick but salvation was impossible—we were too far out into the channel to either get a Tirfor connected or to get ashore. We were marooned and it was getting dark.

I was disappointed with something Nick suggested, which seemed to sum up the whole problem with BW. Nick, who had worked for BW for 14 years, helpfully volunteered to have a go at getting us off there, which would leave us heading in darkness into a fast-flowing and extremely twisty section of river with a lot of overhanging trees. I asked him where he thought I could go. 'Well, find somewhere to tie up,' he said. 'Where exactly?' I asked. 'I don't know,' he replied, shaking his head. I got the impression that he was getting a bit fed up with me, but I was unhappy being sent headlong into the unknown, in the dark, with who-knows-what consequences.

We were finally freed at 4pm the following day, after BW resorted to hiring a 38-ton wrecker—the sort of thing that tows stranded HGVs off the motorway. Scragg rowed off with lines in the dinghy which were attached to a hook on the truck. After four or five pulls and two broken ropes, that idea was abandoned. The lorry driver provided a couple of heavy-duty wire ropes which we attached to the two forward bollards, one each side of the bow. After a few pulls one way and then the other, we slid free. That particular section of river to Burghfield Lock is fraught with all manner of perils; it's very, very tight and has fast-flowing bends, with lots of dangerous overhanging branches strategically placed to sever arteries or take out eyes, usually on the outside of the bends. Attempting that in the dark would have been suicidal. Nick agreed they should have been cut back but said there'd been no time because of the foot-and-mouth disease outbreak. Ironically, I noticed signs at several locks warning of wet paint.

Although I didn't particularly want to stop, we'd had enough by the time we reached the Cunning Man. It could have been worse though; they did still sell draught Guinness. That evening I had a chat with Norman Briggs, another of the original pioneers on the restored K&A and we decided to tackle the Reading bit backwards. By an ironic twist the new edition of the annual Kennet & Avon Yearbook, published by BW, had arrived and I was amused to read, under the heading Boat Dimensions, that the maximum width and minimum maintained depth were 14ft and 3ft 7in respectively, although they qualified this by saying the minimum depth would be achieved after the completion of a backlog of dredging. From my experience, that meant an awful lot of dredging! Some friends who lived nearby, Jerry and Jenny, came to the pub and Jenny offered to drive us into Reading so we could look at the amount of flow through the narrow walled section running through the centre of town, known as the Brewery Gut. We could see that the flow had certainly subsided, and I thought it was probably gentle enough to go through forwards and so save buggering about below the lock, but we would have a better idea when we got there. It was certainly useful to have had the chance to look at the situation in advance.

But it still wasn't all over; the canal had a couple of final tricks to play. On pushing off from the Cunning Man, we stuck again almost immediately after passing through Burghfield Bridge. We managed to clear this with a tow from a friendly resident narrowboat tug for the price of a bottle of Cab Sauv—bargain! At Reading it started to rain, and we moored under the road bridge above County Lock to avoid having to reassemble the wheelhouse.

While we were there, I decided we may as well turn around, ready to go into the lock astern. I thought I'd be clever and let the current turn the boat while holding on a head-rope tied ashore. That was a mistake and we jammed sideways across the Cut. Having cleared that, I reverted to Plan A and moved into the lock facing forward. As the lock emptied, we rubbed the bottom and had to flush ourselves out.

By this time a couple of upstream boats had arrived and were waiting in the stream to enter the lock. We got the green light to proceed, took a deep breath and went for it. Everything looked fine as we approached the skewed Highbridge (which isn't at all—skewed yes, but high?). It was an arched affair rather like the one at Newbury except that it had the added complication of being on an angle and no floating fenders. It was absolutely essential that we lined up exactly central in order to clear the brick sides. I aimed slightly to the right, intending to swing the stern into the flow. All looked well until at the very last minute the stern bucked and swung to port as we rode over a submerged and solid object. I threw the engine astern and the boat shuddered to a stop before the folded wheelhouse windows made contact with the brick of the arch.

The stern came to rest in a forest of overhanging trees with strong and potentially lethal branches. We could not move either way: the stern was jammed into the bank and the other end was resting against the sides of the bridge. I cursed the submerged shopping trolley and Scragg risked death by crushing—50 tons of steel and a brick bridge would make short work of a human frame—while we thought about how the hell to get out of it. A large crowd had gathered of course—it was a Saturday. Scragg asked later why so many people had suddenly appeared, and I likened it to the crowds that rubberneck motorway accidents. However, we put some of them to good use. Four or five pushed with the shaft on the port quarter while another half a dozen or so heaved on a rope we'd managed to get across the bridge to the far bank. This had the desired effect and the stern gradually floated into the centre of the channel. I got the bow out into the middle with the bow thrusters and suddenly we were lined up perfectly for the bridge hole. I opened the throttle, Craig and Malcolm reeled in the stern line as quickly as they could to keep it out of the prop and like a cork out of a bottle, we popped out of the other side into the transformed world of the Oracle Shopping Centre. We were there—we had done it! There was a drunk on the towpath who had missed all the fun. 'Thash a nice boat, mate—thash one a them Dush Barshes innit,' he slurred. There was nothing for it but to tie up at Blakes Lock and go for a pint.

Nil illegitimi venturi, as the saying goes. We left Saul Trader tied above Blakes Lock and made for the bar of the Fisherman's Cottage. I intended to check with the lock keeper for permission but as we passed his office, I saw him sprawled across the desk rapt in the arms of Morpheus—dead to the world—and I didn't have the heart to disturb him. We got the Guinness in and sat in the bay window where we could keep an eye on the boat. Halfway down the pint I noticed the lockie leave the cabin, stroll along to the boat, peer in the direction of the wheelhouse and return to the office. Five minutes later he came back out and made a beeline for the pub. He looked straight at us, ensconced sheepishly in the corner. 'That yours?' he said, cocking his head. 'Yes,' I replied, almost apologetically. 'Finish up,' he said bluntly, nodding towards the Guinness. 'Finish up.' I half expected handcuffs to come out and be marched to the assizes. I couldn't remember whether Reading still had a gaol. 'Er, am I in the way then?" I ventured, stalling for time. 'You're moored in a layby and it's against the byelaws.' The layby, of course. You don't get laybys on the cut. We were now under the jurisdiction of the mighty Environment Agency (EA). 'I was about to see you about a licence anyway," I said. I didn't want to tell the whole pub he'd been sound-o on duty. His mood mellowed a little at that. 'Don't give yourselves the hiccups,' he responded. 'Five minutes'll do.'

Blakes Lock is the only one operated by the EA not actually on the River Thames, and the licensing arrangements are an absolute pig's ear. If I was, at times, inclined to think of BW as being a little bit intransigent, then try the EA. I could have a licence for any single day, or one week, or one month. 'I might stay for two months," I told him, "can I pay for one now and the second if I need it?' 'Nope. The maximum is one month and if you go over by as much as one day, you'll be fined £1,000 and charged for an annual licence on top.' I settled for the month; at £190 it was not unduly steep, about the same as an annual licence for the whole of France, but I was puzzled by the total lack of flexibility. The numbers of pleasure boats using the river had declined dramatically over the past ten years. It was a shame because the river had a lot to offer, but from a purely selfish point of view it was marvellous—no queues at the locks and the subsequent procession to the next. It was time for the Thames.

Chapter 4

The River Thames

I T WAS worth the 190 quid just to get some water underneath. I could switch on the depth sounder again—eight, nine, 10ft under the keel... now we were living. We had a month to use as a shakedown before the Channel crossing. We turned left and headed for Oxford, dreaming of spires. Mooring on the Thames had never been particularly easy, even with a narrowboat, but with a barge drawing 3ft 6in it was even more fraught. Below Pangbourne all the official moorings were taken, and I suppose on reflection it was stupid to attempt to get in beside a notice clearly stating mooring was prohibited. We grounded noisily on a submerged concrete ledge and it took some frenzied thrashing to get back off. I remembered mooring here with my narrowboat, Wat Tyler, several years before. Again, space was limited, and I took the liberty of mooring with about 6ft of the bow overhanging a 'no mooring' post. A little old man came along and told me to move. 'You're parked in a prohibited space,' he pointed out. I protested that there was nowhere else, and he took out a notebook and proceeded to scribble a note. 'You'll be 'earing from Pangbourne Parish Council—Mr Tyler,' he said severely. 'I've got your name.' As far as I know, Mr Tyler was never contacted.

The next day we had a short run to Goring, and sampled the hospitality of the John Barleycorn, excellent food in the Catherine Wheel, and a very good Indian to boot. We could have stayed there for a month and in fact we nearly had to, as on returning to the boat in the small hours we found all the domestic batteries as flat as a proverbial pancake. It was a bit like the power cuts of the 1970s; you don't realise how much you depend on electricity until you haven't got any. On a boat the problems are worse as things like water pumps and toilet flush systems rely on the stuff. We could survive though. There was enough candle power to see our way to bed and gas cooking, but having to ablute, make coffee and wash up using water cans was a bit too close to Scout camps for my liking. The battery charger would not kick in either, as by a trick of modern technology, its brain was so bloody clever that when the batteries were totally flat it didn't recognise the fact that there were any at all, and therefore didn't think it needed to do any charging.

The lock keeper at Goring recommended Haynes Auto Electrical, a firm at Wallingford. Luckily, the engine start batteries were still OK, so we headed in that direction. Haynes said their mobile lecky, Andy, was busy for several days but would get down as soon as he could. Another night was spent in a Victorian gloom and we were starting to smell a bit, wondering whether Wallingford had any public baths. I was sitting in the wheelhouse at 7.30am with a bowl of muesli and warm, curdled milk when I became aware of a shape outside the window. I saw a boiler-suited, shaven-haired lad with a big grin animatedly waving his arms up and down. Andy. He had a couple of spare hours and came to see what he could do. Bless him!

Andy was brilliant, and in a matter of minutes he was at it with his tester. By 9am he emerged, still with the same huge grin, and announced, 'Absolutely shot to bloody pieces.' Well, they had been in there for more than five years and I'm not exactly careful with my battery maintenance ('white man's magic,' as Phil Trotter would say). Andy was such a nice bloke that I parted with the large cheque almost without feeling any pain. Wallingford was that sort of place. Everybody was so pleasant that you hardly noticed when they came around each day and took eight quid for the mooring. Later on, I had occasion to leave the boat there. I telephoned the borough council to explain and the phone was answered by no less than the town clerk himself. 'No problem. If you don't see the mooring clerk when you leave, just put a cheque in the post, that'll be OK.' It goes without saying that I did just that.

As we had a bit of time, I decided to explore some of the navigable backwaters. One was the weir stream that bypassed Clifton Lock and led to Long Wittenham, and I asked the lock keeper whether there would be enough depth. 'Don't see why not,' he said cheerily, "you've got to have a go haven't you—if you get stuck, you'll be there until next winter but the pub's good.' We bumped the bottom a few times but nothing too dramatic occurred. The Plough was indeed good with a little landing stage at the bottom of the garden, just long enough for us. They held regular folk music nights and had an Aunt Sally team, a game peculiar to Oxfordshire, I think, where you throw sticks at a skittle perched on top of a pole. One of the rules states that if the skittle is dislodged by contact with the pole rather than the skittle itself, a point may be awarded at the discretion of the umpire, a situation I imagine could lead to a fair bit of controversy after a few pints—especially as the umpire is usually from the home pub! Another good reason for visiting Long Wittenham was the Pendon Museum, housing a wonderful exhibition of rural England in the days of the Great Western Railway of the 1930s, depicted in minutely detailed miniature. There were oo model railways and superbly crafted buildings, many of which were furnished in immaculate detail.

Over the next couple of weeks, we called at Abingdon where we met Harry the Cobbler, who insisted on showing us some of the sights, one of which was a pub that stayed open until everyone had finished drinking. In the morning we struggled to get up to make our way at the appointed time of 8am to view Harry's 'Dickensian workshop' but unfortunately Harry didn't show up! We then spent a couple of nights in Oxford before starting the downstream run towards Teddington and the tideway. The boat was behaving again, and I was looking forward to the Channel crossing with renewed confidence.

The tides were decreasing to Neaps by the following weekend. The weather forecast was not encouraging; South Westerly force 4-5 and a bit unsettled. Ever the optimists, we continued down river. We bunkered at Reading with 300 gallons of red diesel (France do not offer this luxury) and made Marlow by early evening. Once again, no moorings—I ran aground looking for a spot among the private and keep off signs decorating the banks. There was just one vacant spot, outside the haughty looking grounds of the Compleat Angler Hotel and below the elegant Marlow Suspension Bridge. I took the precaution of telephoning to obtain permission to moor, on the understanding that we would of course be dining in the hotel. We showered quickly and made ourselves as respectable as boaters can before going in for pre-dinner drinks. No Guinness so we settled for two halves of lager and a G&T. The waiter brought the bill on an ominous-looking silver tray and asked, 'Who is the host, sir?' 'I don't know about host but I'm in charge of the kitty. How much do you want?' It was £13.95. We were out of there before he'd brought the 5p change! We settled for a takeaway pizza for dinner. The following morning as we left the mooring, someone officious looking in a dark suit came striding across the lawn. Sensing his mission, I immediately let go aft and engaged bow thruster, putting a respectable distance between us. He wanted to know whether we had permission to tie there. Apparently, the usual charge is equivalent to half the room rate, and we didn't stop to find out what that was! Mary Shelley wrote Frankenstein in Marlow—this could've quite easily turned into another horror story for us and the kitty.

The following night we tied at the Anglers at Walton for free. While we were there someone wanted to watch the Wimbledon Men's Tennis Final. My TV did not see the light of day very often, just the odd Grand Prix or Match of the Day now and again. I had never had much joy with the reception either. I'd tried various expensive antennae and boosters, but nothing seemed particularly consistent. Consequently, I was now down to a glorified coat hanger, which seemed to be just as effective as anything else. On this particular day however it wouldn't find a picture inside or outside the boat, and I eventually managed a sort of zig-zaggy conglomeration of shapes that looked like dancers at a strobe disco alternating between black and white and a sort-of colour. While all this was going on my mobile rang. It was a friend, John Baldry, who pilots cruise ships through the Glacier Bay off the coast of Alaska. He was calling from Ketchikan and the signal was crystal clear. 'That's brilliant that is though isn't it,' said Scragg philosophically, 'you can speak to someone on the other side of the world and you can't get the tennis from ten miles down the bloody road. You cannot be serious!'

The weather had not really improved, and the forecast still sounded grim. The numbers five and six were used a bit too often for my liking in relation to the wind force. Saul Trader would probably be OK in a four or even a five at a push (Duncan once said he would go anywhere with it) but it would be extremely uncomfortable, and it seemed sensible to wait for a calmer spell. Someone I had met in Gloucester Docks, Colin Jones, with the barge Libertas, was having some work done in a small boatyard near Hampton Court. We decided to pay him a visit and I was really pleased we did. Not only did we manage to get the broken stanchions from the little accident at Newbury re-welded (all for £35), but we discovered another world, a Lilliputian world called Platts Eyot.

The boat sheds and slip there are now listed buildings as they were used for the construction of Fast Patrol vessels during the Second World War. Platts Eyot is connected to the mainland via a very narrow bridge with a tight right-angled bend at each end. The access is so tight that the only vehicles that can reach the island are the tiny Bedford Rascal/Suzuki Carry vans, and all deliveries have to transhipped before they can be taken to the island. Consequently, there are scores of these little vans and trucks buzzing around, most of them with large gouges and dents in their sides where they haven't quite judged the gaps and scraped the bridge. There were vans, trucks, tippers, flatbeds, minibuses… it was like something out of Gulliver's Travels. We half expected to be confronted by armies of people 3ft tall and with squeaky voices.

The next day the forecast we had been hoping for finally arrived. Winds SE force 2-3, visibility moderate, seas slight. We were going for it.

Chapter 5

The Thames to Calais

I TELEPHONED THE River Thames hotline to get the tide times for Teddington Lock. 'Where exactly is that?' was the first question. 'Er, in Teddington,' I explained, 'probably the most important lock on the river where the canalised section joins the tidal Thames.' 'So—sorry—you want a locksmith in Toddington?'

I believe the EA emergency line was at that time operated by the Warwickshire Ambulance Service or some such, and after a few more similar questions I gave up and rang Duncan. He ran Aquatech, a marine support service providing technical support from a highly sophisticated semi-rigid inflatable which he built himself from scratch in a shed in Frampton on Severn and which he dragged around the world behind an ex-NATO Mercedes 10-ton Unimog. Duncan is one of the cleverest blokes I know;

he also designed computer programmes (Aquatech 2 was packed with elaborate systems and could hold the boat on a position with around 6in of leeway) and he designed an amazing underwater camera that took pictures of the seabed, reproducing them instantaneously on a screen in the boat. Duncan is a bloody genius, but like a lot of genii, his top priority is not financial acumen. His lovely wife Sheila looks after all that. Although he is always busy, he had kindly agreed to take a couple of days off and do the crossing with us. He didn't take a lot of persuading, to be honest.

I had been told that Dutch Barges making the crossing sometimes tied overnight alongside the old Radio Caroline ship, the Ross Revenge, at Queenborough in the mouth of the Medway, so I sent an email to the website to ask whether this would be possible. Peter Moore replied saying we would be welcome to lie alongside and suggested we contact André, the vessel's caretaker, to let him know. It ended with a note of caution. 'Under no circumstances go drinking with André unless you are prepared for a very long night! Only drink with André on the homeward run. Many a good ship has been sunk because the crew were pissed. Best wishes, Peter.' It sounded like a bit of a challenge.

Before we were in a position to cross that particular bridge however, there was another challenge lurking around the corner, or in this case, in the very next lock cut. On the approach to Sunbury Lock, the very evening before we were due to start our intrepid voyage to France, the engine cut out and died. Luckily, we were out of the flow of the current and after a bit of bleeding (and cursing) and bleeding cursing, it burst into life again, just long enough for us to get into the lock where it gave up the ghost for good. After the lock had been lowered, we bow-hauled the boat on to the pontoon and Roy, my practical brother, dived below again. He stripped down the fuel pump and cleaned the filter—nothing. We had fuel in the secondary filters, but we could get none out of the tank. Roy was beginning to tear his hair out (what was left of it) and blamed himself for damaging the diaphragm. After another four or five strip-downs we were beginning to get desperate. We were unlikely to get spares at 8pm on a Saturday. Why do these things always happen at weekends and bloody Bank Holidays? I had warned Duncan of our problem—he had to come from Gloucester, and I didn't want him making the journey for nothing.

As a last resort Roy thought of checking the supply pipe from the tank, a braided rubber tube that connected the tank to the priming pump. He put it into a bucket of water and blew down the end and the bucket filled with bubbles. The pipe had split, and it wasn't the pump at all. By now it was 10pm. I phoned Duncan again to tell him what was going on, but he was already on his way. He arrived at 11.30pm armed with a large crate of pumps, fittings, pipes and tubes and guided by a map on his laptop connected to a GPS resting in the windscreen. He had enough spare parts with him to rebuild the engine and in less than an hour we were running again. Surely Saul Trader had now performed its last cunning stunt. We were under way at 8am and heading for Teddington Lock, the last non-tidal link before France. The engine was running sweetly, although I wouldn't have dared mention that at the time! We would be pushing the tide for the first couple of hours and it crossed my mind that if the engine did fail again, at least we would drift slowly back to Teddington. But as we left and motored into the tideway, the motor settled into a confident and reassuring rhythm.

Duncan had rigged up the GPS to his laptop and although it was still programmed to autoroute, as his chart disc did not cover the upper reaches of the Thames, we followed our steady progress as a black line on the screen showed us passing Richmond and Eel Pie Island, then the entrance to the Grand Union Canal at Brentford, Kew Gardens and Chiswick and on to the familiar bridges associated with the University Boat Race—Hammersmith, Fulham, Putney, Wandsworth—and on past the imposing remnants of the Battersea Power Station. The tide turned and was pushing us along at a great rate so that by the time we passed beneath the ornate Albert Suspension Bridge we were clocking 8 knots. Through the centre of London, we were fairly flying. The traffic intensified and created a confused maelstrom of lumping wash, so there was no time to gaze at the famous land-marks, and certainly no place to break down.

There was the Houses of Parliament, and the London Eye bending its weary circle, Waterloo Bridge rattling with commuter trains, London Bridge and the Pool, where we reported to the Port of London Control for permission to proceed. Ferries ploughed to and fro, seem-ingly oblivious to the rule of the road. At one stage a fire tug, pushing up a 6ft tidal wave, crashed past. On we swept, passing below the railway bridges of Waterloo and Blackfriars, the 'wobbly' bridge, (still wobbling at that time), the majestic Tower Bridge and St Kathar-ine's Dock, and Limehouse where the Regent's Canal and River Lee join the Thames. Then King George Fifth Dock from where I had sailed many years ago to the Far East aboard the Pando Head, courtesy of the Peninsular & Oriental Steam Navigation Co. Evocative names that conjured days of contraband and piracy, of exotic cargoes landed from sailing ships from exotic places—East India Dock, the Isle of Dogs—Canning Town and The Pros-pect of Whitby. So much to see and so little time, all our concentration absorbed in ensuring a safe passage through the chaos.

The traffic subsided a little and we checked in with Woolwich Radio for permission to transit the Thames Barrier. 'Saul Trader—Saul Trader—Charlie Span,' came the terse reply. Not some secret agent but the gap in the barrier that we were to pass through. Strangely the spans seemed to be numbered rather than lettered, but two bright green lights clearly indicated the opening and suddenly we were out into the wild, London a mere distant shimmer. We were now in the company of real sea-going ships. Duncan swapped the autoroute with a proper chart. We were buoy-hopping now and almost at sea. The entrance to the Medway involves a long wide sweep around the Isle of Grain and it was nearly 7pm when we sighted the unmistakable red hulk of the Ross Revenge, our haven for the night. We were secured along-side by 8pm and there was no sign of André, just as well really as we were all far too knackered even for a run ashore in the dinghy. We had a couple of cans and a fry-up and were turned in by 10am. There was another long day ahead.

I was awoken at 6am by a violent lurching motion and leapt up to see a huge ocean-going tug ploughing past, presumably on her way to shepherd a giant container ship into the port of Tilbury. The day dawned as one of those rare, perfectly still summer mornings, with the sea an oily calm and the shriek of the gulls penetrating the tangy air. Perfect. After bacon rolls, we cast off at 8am to push the last couple of hours of the flood tide along the North Kent Coast. Duncan had elected to take the inshore course through the narrow Gore Channel, pass-ing close to Margate before heading for Calais, leaving the Goodwin Sands to the south. When I had looked at it earlier, I'd envisaged staying out in the main Princes

Channel and then turning south to pass inside the Good-wins to Ramsgate, which would have provided a shelter if needed. As it happened, the forecast was settled for the next 48 hours, and by keeping to the north we avoided the busy ferry routes with their attendant wash. Furthermore, the Gore Channel, which had looked to me from the chart to be about half an inch wide, was of course several hundred yards and gave us more than enough water at this state of the tide. We passed the ghostly tattered masts of wrecks jutting eerily into the haze off the Red Sands Towers as a procession of container ships ploughed past, busily coming and going with their stacks of steel boxes.

Once into the Channel proper, the sea was as calm as a lake and almost an anti-climax. Saul Trader took what little swell there was in its stride, as though she'd been at sea all her life. We crossed a few ships in the separation lanes, changing course a couple of times to give way to eastbound freighters, and the only slightly hairy moment came when we were hit abeam by a 10ft wash that rocked us violently half a dozen times and sent the laptop sliding across the wheelhouse table and perilously close to going over the side. There was an almighty crash from below and I thought that the TV had burst out of its cabinet on to the deck. When we recovered, it turned out that the cutlery drawer had slid out of its runners and dumped its contents on to the galley deck. We never saw the offending vessel and assumed it must have been a distant SeaCat doing 40-odd knots. Duncan reckoned it must have been at least five miles away and I certainly wouldn't have wanted to be much closer. After a couple of hours, the coast of England had disappeared and replaced by the coast of France, and at about 5.30pm we triumphantly hoisted the tricolour as we entered French territorial waters.

Getting into Calais was a bit like landing at Heathrow. We lurked around outside the entrance for an hour or so while four ferries and a SeaCat sailed and another three arrived. We listened on the VHF as they navigated in an out of the port. 'Normandie, Normandie, this is Pride of Dover. Pass me green to green please over.' Then from Calais Port Control at last, 'Saul Tradeur Saul Tradeur. Ze surd feery ees ze Sea France Renoir—you can follow eem—over. And quickly pleese.' Ten minutes later we were safely inside the entrance and tied to the Fish Wharf to await the lock for the Bassin de L'Oeust. We were on the 10.15pm ferry back to Dover. Bon Soir France and 'ello England.

'Step this way please sir.' Would you believe it? Half past midnight at Dover and each of the foot passengers, five in total with one bag apiece, was pulled over by Her Majesty's Customs & Excise. 'Where've you been, why, where are you going, what for, how long…?' I really didn't need this after an 18-hour day with the prospect of another four or five-hour drive ahead. Of course, they found nothing. Duncan's theory was that they rummaged about while asking the questions to watch for any reaction giving away that your toothpaste is pure heroin and you have 30 packets of Old Holborn stuffed up your back-side. The fifth lad they had stopped, a Scouser, had been screaming abuse all the while, colourfully telling the excise men their life history. 'I think he's a spokesman for all of us,' I remarked, when they finally let me go. When we got outside Duncan said nonchalantly, 'They didn't even mention the six rocket flares I've got in my bag!'

Chapter 6

Sur le Continent... At Last

WE RETURNED to Calais three weeks later. As we walked from the ferry into the terminus building as second-class citizens—or as the ferry companies called us, foot passengers—I couldn't help feeling a bit concerned. It was almost midnight. Would the boat still be there? Would it be bare of all internal fittings, stripped ruthlessly by gangs?

I needn't have worried; Saul Trader was there exactly as we'd left it. Nothing had changed—apart from the fact that the tide was 6ft lower than it was when we left and there was no ladder and no way that any of us geriatrics were going to leap that far into the black of the night. Fortunately, we had Scragg. He'd only made the trip by the skin of his teeth. Born in Stonehouse he had never ventured further than Gloucester in all his 28 years.

Getting a passport was like completing the Appellation Way to him. We had given him the forms three times, and he spoiled the first two. I told him his photograph would need to be validated by someone of authority, quietly doubting whether he actually knew anyone of authority, let alone anyone who would vouch for him! 'Oil go and see the Fat Policeman then,' he said.

Then he had to get a day off work to go to the Passport Office in Newport. Getting a day off from RWD was not an easy task. I was in the office once when one of the lads came in, obviously on his knees with flu. 'Sorry Phil," he snorted, covering his face with a snotty bit of oily rag, 'I won't be in tomorrow.' That was it. Phil started on a withering tirade in his deadpan Potteries spiel. 'That's bloody great that is,' he said, 'do you know how long they've been trying to find a cure for flu, Runt? Bloody years. The best brains in the world having been trying to find a cure and you've managed to find one yourself in a couple of hours. Bloody fantastic that—'ave a bloody day off. You should write to the British Medical Journal you should—a cure for flu is found by some twat from a boatyard in Gloucestershire. Bloody fantastic.' Runt backed down. Phil never gave the luxury of a counter-opinion; if he said black was white, then you just had to believe it. 'Alright Phil, I'll see how it is in the morning.' Scragg was luckier. Having got the day off, he was within ten minutes of the passport office when he realised he'd forgotten his birth certificate—and had to go all the way back to Gloucester for it.

'I'm certainly not going down there,' I announced, looking into the gloom as we stood like lemons beside our baggage on the quayside. 'You've gone wimp 'aven't you?' said Scragg, peering over the edge. He had a turn of phrase that's unique to him, did Scragg. 'After you then,' I replied, gently nudging him over the edge. He landed several seconds later, unharmed on the hatch. We laid the gangplank across the gap on to the wheelhouse roof for the geriatrics: Mick, 40 years before the mast in Her Majesty's Cable Ships, and a brass and ropework an obsession; Malcolm, ex-P&O printer with a serious deteriorating eye condition that had left him partially sighted but who had perfected the art of lassoing bollards from a Tam & Di Murrell video; and me. We tiptoed precariously aboard to an encouraging tirade of 'wimps!' from Scragg. Motley was a word that came to mind.

The following day the tidal gate was opened in the afternoon, which gave us a chance to get the boat cleaned up and explore the town. I went to the VHF office to get my French vignette, but it was closed. I had picked up all sorts of warnings from various soothsayers about cruising in France. 'They'll confiscate all your fresh meat', and 'No dairy products or vegetables are allowed', and 'You'll need a VHF licence, ships registration papers, VAT receipts, international certificate of competence etc, etc' and 'You can't have a wheel with exposed spokes'. In the event nobody whatsoever came aboard or asked for any documents, even passports. It was almost an anti-climax and I thought it couldn't possibly last. They didn't even ask to see Scragg's passport, which quite upset him. 'What's the point of having one if they don't even look at it then?'

We left the inner dock at 5.30pm, motored through a melee of small boats jostling for position and entered the canal. The first lock was open at both ends and we sailed through with a cheery wave from the éclusier. So far so good. I had at least expected to be taken to the Bastille. This French cruising lark was a doddle. The next lock was a hundred yards or so around the corner. I looked through the binoculars at the little concrete cabin which was firmly closed. There was no sign of any activity. What do we do now then? There was a small English yacht tied on the wall. The skipper told us he'd been waiting since 6am! I found the VHF channel in the Carte Guide and called Port Control. 'Ee will be 'ere in 20 minute,' was the response. 'That's what he told me this morning,' said the yacht skipper. An hour later I radioed again. It was now getting on for 7pm. 'Ee will be 'ere in 20 minute.' Shortly afterwards another boat arrived, flying a French flag astern. Would this change things? Within minutes a ubiquitous white van came tearing across the bridge, screeched to a halt at the lock and almost immediately the gates opened. Voila!

'Can I get a licence here?' I asked, pre-empting the inevitable. 'Non, non, le bureau ferme.' Tomorrow was Sunday—'Lundi Monsieur, Lundi.' I didn't fancy hanging around until Lundi so we carried on. There was another

VNF office in Dunkirk and if necessary, I would plead ignorance. The following morning, we followed the French boat into the Canal du Calais. There were a number of manned lift bridges and I wasn't sure whether they opened on Sundays, so it was a case of 'when in France'. Sure enough, one by one the bridges opened, and the bridge keepers waved as we passed without a hint of 'who do you think you are getting me out on a Sunday?' We soon left Calais behind and settled down to enjoy the hospitality of France. Shortly we got the first shaking fist and tirade in French from a bank-side fisherman. 'Bloody fishermen—same all over the world,' observed Scragg.

Dunkirk was unexciting. We tied up apprehensively in a seedy-looking area beneath the railway where sleek TGVs slid past. On a Sunday in Dunkirk it was virtually impossible to buy a cigar, and anything else for that matter. I toured the streets before finding the only Tabac that was open. The next morning, we diverted on to the short branch to Bergues, a delightful little walled town about nine miles to the south. We wandered around the narrow streets and sat outside a small café and drank beer. The temperature was in the high 20s and we tried out the new wheelhouse canopy, which was fine when we stopped but swayed worryingly in the wind when underway. I eventually gave it away; something I came to regret when we reached the south of France.

We crossed the border into Belgium at Adinkerke and stocked up with cigars at a quarter of the UK price in a little town that never closes. Known as Tobacco City, it was crawling with small-time smugglers (most of them British), all eager to risk having their cars confiscated for a few hundred quid profit. It was 7pm when we got to Veurne. We passed another British barge, the Actief, which belonged to Baliol Fowden, a marine surveyor and one of the founders of the Barge Association, but there was no sign of life aboard. One problem with Belgium is that they seem to have at least two names for everything. Here Furnes was the French name and Veurne the Belge. The lock looked closed. I started to turn in to the basin, filled with Dutch steel cruisers, when the lock keeper appeared, waving frantically. Johann welcomed us with open arms and excellent English, delivered in that unique Flemish way, and like everyone we met in Belgium, he was pleased to see us and eager to help. 'You can stay here for two daish. It ish for free.'

The freshwater tap was alongside the lock and we needed a couple of hundred gallons. 'No problem,' beamed Johann, struggling to pull out the hose. 'You can stay for long time here—I mush closhe at midnight the lock.' The pontoon was exactly the right length and as we approached, Malcolm stood poised on the foc'sle, anxious to show off his stuff with the lasso. All his attention focused on the exercise. He squinted at the pontoon, patiently waiting for the bollard to come into his limited line of sight, and then at exactly at the right moment he sent the rope's eye in a perfect looping arc at his target with a nonchalant flick of the wrist. Unfortunately, Scragg appeared at the same moment to take the line from him and the eye passed perfectly over his head. With an automatic reaction, Malcolm jerked on the line to take up the strain, unaware, and with a feeble squeak and a belated 'oi!', Scragg wobbled, lost his balance and was pulled sharply into the cut. 'It's noice in 'ere,' he spluttered as he came to the surface, 'chuck the shampoo.'

Furnes is a beautiful town in the province of West Flanders. A travelling fair was set up in the Market Square (the Grote Markt), all bustle and colour and noise, and we sat outside a corner bar and watched the world go by. Several Renaissance-style buildings, including the 15th century town hall, known as the Spanish Pavilion, and the church of Sint-Niklaas surround the square, which is one of the finest in Belgium. Families were out for the evening and we noticed the refreshing attitude and appearance of the children. They were clean and tidy, and quiet and respectful. Even the teenagers were seemingly unaffected with the boorish lout-style culture we often endure in Britain.

I have a habit of getting names mixed up. It's not dyslexia (never could spell that!), more ol' timers' disease, I suspect. Scragg loved to have a go at me about it. I kept referring to Johann, the lock keeper, as Jonah. 'Why do you keep calling him Jonah?" said Scragg, 'you said the towns have two names, so I suppose the lock keepers do too.' We stayed in Furnes for a couple of days and I had to take the ship's registration papers to Jonah/Johann and sort out the licence for Belgium. For three months the cost was 2,000 Belgian francs (about £30). This covered the whole of the Flemish waterway system and with ample moorings, manned locks and bridges and often free water and electricity, it rather gave the £190 I'd paid for one month on the River Thames the smack of the Great British Rip-Off.

While we were in Furnes, one of the plumbing fittings developed a leak. I'd noticed some pipes being delivered to what seemed like a small builders' lock-up on the quayside, so we decided to see whether there was any chance of finding the bit we required, As the shutter was closed, I rang the bell and we were let in without a word to a small shed with a few shelves of plastic pipes. I thought we were going to be out of luck but then the man who'd let us in pointed to a plastic curtain. On the other side, a whole new world opened. We had inadvertently entered by the delivery door of the Delva Shopping Centre—a real Aladdin's cave of a place that stocked absolutely everything: screws, stationery, crockery, plumbing and electrical stores, ironmongery, toys, plant, motor spares, tools and more. We spent more than an hour rummaging on the three floors. There was absolutely everything you could ever want in there except, that is, the fitting that I was looking for.

The next day we made a 140-degree turn opposite the lock, waved our farewells to Jonah/Johann and followed the small gauge Canal de Lo towards Ypres. That evening we encountered one of the few disadvantages of boating in Europe. The éclusiers follow you everywhere, skittling along in their little vans to open bridges and locks. Sometimes they will ask you to wait for maybe an hour to allow another vessel to pass or catch up and share the locks. This is fine but when they finish for the evening, so do you—wherever you happen to be. On this occasion we were about five miles and two locks from our intended destination at Ypres. Even though there was still a good three hours of daylight remaining we had to tie up in the middle of nowhere and (God forbid) cook for ourselves. The omnipresent éclusier can become a bit restrictive. The freedom of movement enjoyed on the English canals is completely lost; he wants to know when you are going to leave in the morning, where you are going and whether you will be stopping en route, so he and his colleagues down the line can plan their day.

Ypres is another charming town. Mooring was £3.50 per night including water and electricity, and close to the town centre. The town was virtually destroyed during the First World War and was completely rebuilt. On the beautifully imposing Market Square, there were lively bars and a deeply emotive exhibition depicting the role of the town and the surrounding area during the war. At sunset each day, the Last Post was sounded at the Menin Gate in an incredibly moving ceremony.

We completed the ring from Ypres, turning right on to the River Yser, passing through Diksmude and on to Nieuwpoort, where the Yser flows out to sea. On the approach to Nieuwport the canal opened out into a large recreational lake, at the far side of which stood the lock—of monolithic proportions with massive guillotine gates towering overhead. I continued straight on into what seemed like a dead arm with no possibility of turning. The crew looked bewildered. Cunningly, I had some inside information about a perfect mooring.

There was a very good little guide produced by Geoff & Di Bradshaw, available through the Dutch Barge Association for a fiver. It told me there was a pontoon jetty close to shops and bars at the far end and opposite a turning place, and that was where we moored. It was here that we met up for the first time with officialdom. A couple of very polite policemen in a van pulled up and came aboard as soon as we had secured the ropes. They checked our papers and licence, filled in a form and told us that if we were ever asked again, we only need show the form to prove that we had already been 'done.' Then they departed, diplomatically, refusing our offer of a beer. In the evening we took the tram to the seafront and spent a pleasant couple of hours listening to a pop concert on the beach, as the sun went down over the sea. Scragg did his bit for international relations and chatted up a beautiful local girl on the tram. She showed us where to get off (the tram, that is) and then promptly stifled any lingering thoughts in Scragg's mind by dashing off to meet her boyfriend. 'She was real noice,' Scragg observed.

The next morning, we passed through the monolith—the Jorrisluis. It was so big we could have kept
motoring around in circles inside as it emptied. The
fall was a desultory 3ft! We were lowered into the Plas-
sendale Canal where we joined the large commercial
Ostend-Bruges Canal, which would be churning with
fast-moving enormous commercial vessels bearing down
from all sides. Or maybe it was a vicious rumour; in
the 20km to Bruges we didn't see a single boat. On the
outskirts of Bruges, we were held for a few minutes at
several busy bridges on the perimeter of the town. We
didn't see anyone as the bridges were all controlled from
the distant lock, but we got the distinct feeling that Big
Brother was watching. Then we were signalled into the
large triangular lock. There were a few steel yachts inside
and a 38m barge, the Fleur, converted as a hotel boat for
cycling tours. We asked permission and moored alongside,
careful not to damage the immaculate paintwork. After
15 minutes or so the lock keeper asked us to move to
the other side of the lock for some reason I didn't catch.
Maybe he was bored and thought that the spectacle
of watching an amateur making his barge go sideways
would provide a bit of light relief. I moved Saul Trader
slowly and with furtive use of the bow thruster I managed
to bring it to rest gently on the opposite wall, a manoeu-
vre that seemed to impress the Dutch crews and gave
me an undeserved feeling of the clever dick. Moments
later another 10m Dutch motorboat entered. 'There you

are,' I thought, 'the lock keeper did do it for the sport.' But shortly afterwards the lock entrance filled with a bulk that all but shut out the light. A massive 1,300 tonner slid silently and effortlessly alongside the Fleur, driven by the wife with an inch-perfect and nonchalant precision that paled my performance into insignificance.

We found a mooring just past the lock between two converted commercials, one so large that the centre hold had been turned into a beautiful garden with huge luxuriant ornamental plants that would have graced a Chelsea courtyard townhouse, and with the advantage of a roll-top roof that closed when the weather turned inclement. The wonders of Bruges: chocolates, buzzing waterbuses, Trappist beer, a thousand tourists rushing back to their coaches, museums, crooked terraced streets with multicoloured doorways, awe-inspiring cathedrals and more. We settled for a pint of Guinness in O'Neills! Sassenachs!

For Scragg the next adventure was the journey home, alone with his brand-new passport. Would they believe the Fat Policeman? He had to go back to work. Although RWD produced superb boats, most of their work was concentrated on building narrowboats. Their Northwich Trader class has become an iconic sight around the English cut (I can tell one from half a mile). Phil had a lot of theories of his own and couldn't be persuaded that advertising would ever help sell more boats. That was one of the reasons that no more Dutch barges were built until 15 years after Saul Trader. Hardly anybody knew they built them. Phil didn't help either. When anyone asked to visit the yard to see the work for themselves, he would invariably tell them, 'No problem at all—if you can find us!' One evening Phil's daughter took a call from an obviously serious punter who was interested in a Northwich. 'Bloody brochure collector,' said Phil, 'tell 'im we don't do brochures.'

Scragg's trip involved a train from Bruges to Ostend and then a crossing by SeaCat. The train left at 8am and Scragg left for the ten-minute walk to the station at half past five! 'Oi 'ope they stamp my passport, make it worthwhile getting' it. They will, though, won't they?'

We left at 8.30am and headed for Ghent. There was little to do, there being no locks or bridges for 43km. Mick made use of the time as only old seadogs do, polishing brass and splicing, whipping Englefield clips on to the flag halliards, and dhobeying. Mick always amazed me how he managed to pack two weeks' worth of clothes in to one small holdall. 'One 'ard case and one small grip,' he would say. He would then produce clean shorts and T–shirts day after day like rabbits from hats. Pretty soon the back deck took on the appearance of the backyard of a Bangkok laundry.

After eight hours of cruising, we squeezed Saul Trader past lines of moored pleasure boats and round narrow twisting bends into the very heart of Ghent—this time travelling blind. On this occasion Mrs Bradshaw's notes were not altogether clear. Finally, we reached the point of no return and found that all the moorings were reserved for trip boats. It was early on a Tuesday evening. Maybe the trip boats only operated at weekends. I eyed the inviting wall complete with mooring rings, when a man appeared gesticulating and obviously a mind reader. 'Non, non—impossible.'

Ah—so where is possible? Saul Trader slowly inched through 180 degrees. The gesticulator directed us from the wall to a space outside the Ghent Motorboat & Yacht Club, a space I'd noticed but dismissed as being too small and most definitely too expensive. I was spot-on with both counts. The 'madame' came bustling out of a little office shouting for our ropes. After a bit of to-ing and fro-ing and jostling with the boat in front, we managed to get a couple of ropes ashore. The bow stuck out half-way into the cut and the only way to get off was via a scramble up the wall with the aid of a couple of crumbling footholds in the brick. Still, we could just about get ashore, where madame presented us with the bill of £12 per night, and electricity on the meter. Considering this was slightly more than a whole month's licence I thought it a bit steep. But it was right in the centre of the city, and the words 'choice' and 'Hobson' came to mind. I paid graciously, wondering how much commission the gesticulator would get.

We took the dinghy for a recce and discovered the beautiful Gralei harbour with its amazing buildings. We found some steps where we tied up and made for the nearest bar to fully absorb the splendour of the place. Our mooring was literally a hundred yards from the magnificent Sint-Baafsplein. We sat beneath the imposing elevation of St Bavo's Cathedral, enjoying a superb steak accompanied with the hot Tierenteyn mustard Ghent is well-known for, washed down with copious amounts of an equally superb claret. There was no motor traffic at all in the square (Ghent had the largest car-free city centre in Europe) and we watched idly as the silent articulated low-floor trams swished to a halt, disgorging revellers from the suburbs, and the inoffensive bicycles with their hanging panniers and long-legged riders. Ghent also had some 400km of cycle lanes and in some areas even had their own designated streets.

On the stroll back to the boat we paid the inevitable visit to an Irish bar for a Guinness nightcap. I recognised the music playing through the speakers but couldn't place it, so I asked the barman what it was. 'Dayshall,' he said. At first, I couldn't quite make out what it was he was saying, and then it dawned on me. It was an English folk band, Dansaul from Molton, Northamptonshire. I knew the fiddler, Guy Fletcher, quite well; he'd played at the Saul festival with a folk-rock band called Little Johnny England. Apparently, the band were old favourites in the bar and performed there several times a year. Small world.

From Ghent we headed back out to the Ringvaart, the M25 of the Ghent Belgian canal system. In Belgium, places had names in Flemish and French, which was sometimes a bit confusing. Thus, the River Lys was also the Leie. Having struggled to find the correct colloquial pronunciation for Lys, we then found that Leie was pronounced in an entirely different way. Belgium was divided almost in half by the Flemish in the north and the Walloons in the south, with the imaginary line drawn south of Brussels. Ghent, or Gant or Gent, was Belgium's third largest port even though it was some 30km from the Schelde Estuary. A friendly Dutchman aboard a mirror-finished Lynssen in the lock at Bruges had told us that we must explore the River Lys—and who were we to argue with a Linssen owner (£300,000 for the entry model), so we headed straight across the Ringvaart and on to the Lys. It was certainly a very pretty river. Narrow bends passed small sleepy boat clubs and the properties of the good burghers and lawyers and accountants of Ghent. The only largish vessel we passed was a tourist trip boat of about 250 tons. She held the middle of the channel as we stirred up a cloud of silt on the outside of a sweeping bend. The commercials bypassed this section by taking the Canal de Lys and the two met again at Deinze. We moored here for the night (Mrs Bradshaw advised, 'tie up to roadside crash barriers', which we duly did).

We were tied astern of another small converted barge flying the red ensign, the first we'd seen since arrival in Calais. John, the owner, was heading back to the UK to finish his conversion at Pin Mill on the east coast. He proudly showed us around his boat, so far only lined with plywood. I thought of the amount of work and hours involved in the fitting out of barge and quietly thanked God that mine had been done for me. I am no DIY lover (I really don't have any inclination to be one) but I do admire those who have the skills, patience and dedication to do their own work. As far as I'm concerned, the intricacies of joinery come into the same wow category as the pyramids or Stonehenge or the great religious edifices. The amount of time and patience let alone skill (none of which I have in any quantity) that goes into the finished product, I can only admire. I find it completely impossible to measure a gap, cut a piece of wood, supposedly using exactly the same measurement, and then get that same piece of wood to fit into the gap. I know a lot of people whose boating consists solely of hammering, drilling, measuring and sawing and I take my hat off to them. For me boating is a question of pushing a button, starting the engine, casting off the ropes, and getting underway. Everyone to their own.

At Deinze we found the Gentleman's Club, having declined the only other eating establishment that was open on the grounds that the staff's knowledge of English didn't stretch to gin and tonic. The Gentleman's Club was anything but: no half-naked lap dancers or dodgy looking girls with dodgier looking clients, and certainly no gentlemen! It was a quiet, Formica-topped bar with a smoky card school in one corner and an appetising menu. Maybe we got too carried away. After an excellent prawn curry, Malcolm and I spent most of the night putting the sanitary infrastructure under severe pressure, and the following day half afraid to move!

At Kortrijk (or Courtrai), thanks again to Mrs Bradshaw, we reversed into a disused arm under a very low bridge which the wheelhouse cleared by about 2in, and found ourselves placed for the centre of the town, under the shadow of the 14th century Broel Towers, originally part of the town's defences. We dined (very gently) in Courtrai's classical square and returned early to the boat, dodging a torrential deluge. The next morning, we crept out beneath the low bridge and back into the river, where we needed to turn very sharply right into the bottom lock of the Canal de Bossuit. This may be an appropriate moment to answer anyone who may be critical of the fact that we never stay anywhere very long. There are people (and many have written about their experiences in lengthy tomes) who tie up to a grassy bank and dwell there for days or even weeks on end. We were not like that. For various reasons—time, inclination, preference—we could be more likened to the working boatmen of the English canals, whose motto was 'gotta get 'em on'.

Mick cast us off with his customary shout of 'all queer fore and aft' and went forward to look out for traffic on the move. To our left the river disappeared around to the right, obscuring visibility beyond 300m or so. Mick gave the thumbs-up and I started the turn. Saul Trader, being 21m long, turns almost in its own length with the aid of the bow thruster. Somebody said you could turn it on a sixpence if you had one big enough. It swung around without straddling the main channel. Mick walked casually aft and entered the wheelhouse. 'He gave you a bit of a blast, but I think you were OK!' he remarked. I spun round to see the bows of a 38m empty ploughing past with the current, pushing up a creditable wall of water. It reminded me that nothing can be taken for granted on the cut. When Mick had given me the nod there was nothing in sight. In the time it took to turn Saul Trader through 180 degrees, the Mon Dieu had crashed around the bend, flat out. Had the turn been a little tighter, or God forbid, had the engine faltered, we could have been stranded broadside across his path with consequences that didn't bear thinking about. Expect the unexpected!

Rain persisted throughout the day and we were lucky to have the willing and cheerful assistance of lock keepers, all smiles beneath their waterproof hats, through the 11 locks to Bossuit. Excellent value for a few cans of beer. As usual though in these circumstances, it is impossible to plan a passage. At 1pm the waving of arms and the miming of a hand in front of a mouth taking a bite from a hypothetical sandwich indicated scran time, and so there was nothing for it but to tie up and wait. This ritual never took place at the same time on any stretch and was never for the same duration. Sometimes they would disappear for an hour or more and at others, such as today, they would shout down after about ten minutes, gesticulating towards the next lock. We bolted our baguettes and cheese and restarted the engine. I was always particular about abstaining from alcohol at these times. Apart from the fact that the regulations strictly forbade it, I rigidly enforced the code of sobriety when we were on the move. These were not the narrow canals of England, where one could quite safely shove the gear into neutral, abandon the tiller and dive down below to make a sandwich and a cup of coffee without undue cause for alarm. Here, as I so often discovered, due care and attention was essential, as one literally never knew what was around the next corner.

At the junction with the Bovenschelde Canal at Bossuit, a town not considered worthy of a mention by Mrs B, we turned left and headed north for Oudenaarde. 'A quiet town, famous for its beer—enlivened by its market on Thursday,' said Bristow in the book Through Belgian Canals. It was Wednesday and we were due for a day off. The market was certainly lively, and the annual fair was in town. The River Schelde wound through Oudenaarde in a narrow channel with steep walls on either side. There was a lift bridge carrying the busy Westerring and connecting the two sides of the town, controlled by an equally busy bridge keeper, who anticipated the movement of the massive commercials with such precision that they steamed past flat out with seemingly seconds to spare before the bridge lifted and prevented their wheelhouses getting demolished on the steel structure. This very skilled operation obviously meant inconvenience to the heavy traffic was kept to an absolute minimum but also that the wash from fast-moving 1,350 tonners coming up from France resulted in an uncomfortable mooring for the likes of us.

We were tied to railings and I did not relish this particularly, so we moved through the bridge and found a quiet arm so narrow that we had to reverse in, but with recently installed pontoons with water and electricity laid on, and somewhat flatteringly called the Yachthaven. It was just a few minutes' walk to the market square, dominated by the splendidly flamboyant 16th century town hall. Early the following morning, we replenished our stores from the wonderful market before collapsing with our bulging carrier bags into a wonderful bar called De Carillon, a typically English market square bar with heavily painted shutters and stained glass quarterlights, for a couple of pints of Warsteiner, the consensus being that it was a little too early for the serious Trappist ale the town is famous for. It was frustrating not be able to understand the banter of the market traders with their money purses strapped to their middles, who were earnestly discussing trading conditions, sometimes with a disbelieving throwing up of arms and a creasing frown, and at others with wild cries of laughter. I consoled myself in the belief that the conversation was probably exactly the same as that which could be heard every Tuesday in the Market Inn in Salisbury, or the equivalent of every marketplace in every town in the world. 'Business was terrible' and 'poured with rain just as the schlapper had finished flashing up' and 'had a right nause about 10 o'clock, wanted to exchange a pair of jeans! Told him he needed to speak to the returns department, and they wouldn't be here until next week.'

We had intended to go on to Dendermonde and leave the boat there, but I liked the town and especially the mooring, so much so that we decided to stay where we were. Our friend with the Linssen from Bruges turned up and, possibly pleased that we had taken his advice about the Lys, invited us aboard his superbly expensive vessel for a glass or two. He told us he'd had to replace the glass door to the shower compartment at a cost of £2,500. All very nice but I'd be afraid to use the bloody shower at that price. Through a late-night patronage, we made friends with Marco, the owner of a little burger-and-frites establishment just across the road from the mooring. Marco kindly offered to drive us and our baggage to the railway station on our departure and said he would keep an eye on the boat. In return we promised to bring him a gallon of Sarson's vinegar from England as an alternative to the mayonnaise in which continentals always seem to drown their frites.

When retrieving the car at the end of a trip, we invariably used the train. Belgium apparently had more railway per square mile than any other country in Europe. What's more, it ran on the fascinating principle of clean and efficient, though not necessarily ultra-modern trains, spot-on

The maiden trip with Saul Trader on the Gloucester and Sharpness Canal.

The Wat Tyler.

Saul Trader's saloon.

Roger Hatchard's office in the cottage at Diglis.

The pile of rocks at Limpley Stoke…

175

...And some solace at Bradford-on-Avon.

A tight fit at Waddon Bridge.

Stuck in the middle with you.

At the bottom of the Caen Hill flight of locks - and a blocked filter.

In one end at Bruce Tunnel.

And out of Bruce Tunnel's other side.

The Great Western 6024 King Edward I
hurries a trian through Bradford-on-Avon.

Towney Lock, and a tight fit coming in.

Stuck fast on the way out of Towney Lock.

A quiet early morning outside The Swan.

Mick, Malcolm and Eddie outside The Plough at Long Wittenham.

The Compleat Angler.

Keith aboard the SS Pando Head.

Under the clock in Calais.

'It's noice in 'ere!' says Scragg.

Oudenaarde - the massive commmercials
steam by.

Experimenting with the canopy.

No sooner had we got tied up, a commercial appeared around the bend.

Mick (Scrubber) as busy as ever.

The first sight of the old lifts and the too narrow entrance on the right.

The guillotine gate rose up as a loaded péniche motored slowly out.

Tournai.

Notec, refuelling on the move at Antoing.

Above: Moored below the lock at Herentals.
Below: We were among the big boys!

And suddenly we became the big fish.

Venerable craft at Wolververshaven.

Wolververshaven.

The Crystal Symphony in Amsterdam.

Alongside the quay at Groningen.

Roy and Knocker exploring in the rubber boat.

Scragg modelling the new blue board.

Swimming ladder down!

Under the Windmill at Birdaard.

Moored at Sneek.

The railway lift bridge.

Wedding party aboard!

The Ronquières inclined plane.

Approaching the new lift at Strepy Thieu.

timings and extremely reasonable prices. The journey to Calais took three hours and involved changes at Courtrai and Oostende, costing the equivalent of £8. There were no delays through leaves or snow (no frozen points at Dunton Green), no breakdowns or signal failures and the whole operation passed with a quiet efficiency. We even had the luxury of a seat!

WE DON'T GO FAR BUT WE DO SEE LIFE

.

Chapter 7

Southern Belgium

I T WAS not always easy to find available crew. People had other things to do with their lives, like work. My various friends and eligible crew sometimes had other priorities.

Mick was great. As well as being amusing and good company, he had that unique ships company mentality acquired from 40 years at sea—man and boy. He'd retired from Post Office Cable Ships a few years before and was suffering from serious withdrawal. He invariably jumped at the chance of escaping grass-cutting and decorating. He could splice and whip rope with his eyes closed and he loved to polish brass. When I picked him up with his little yellow CS Alert bag, he came out with the usual quip. 'One 'ard case with one soft grip.' His wife, Vera, quite accustomed to a life of her own while Mick was at sea, was secretly rather glad to get rid of him for a few weeks. She would usually send him off with a kiss and a lovely big Bakewell Tart. 'Don't drop it on your foot,' Mick would joke. 'She said if we don't eat it, we can keep it for a spare anchor.' (Once, in the Cape of Good Hope, I noticed one of the puddings chalked up on the board above the bar read Cherry Bakewell Tart. Some wag had inserted the words 'is a' after Bakewell).

I couldn't think of anything worse than barging with a reluctant crew and wife to boot (if you'll pardon the expression). Saul Trader, at 21m long and 60 tons or so, is small in the company of the 1,500-ton commercials handled with irritating ease by a husband and wife; she steers with inch-perfect precision into the lock while he wanders nonchalantly to the bow to drop the eye of the fore line over the bollard and she takes up the strain with the motor—nothing to it. Two capable crew who can hand reef and steer are an invaluable asset on any boat. There is always something to do; steering, plotting the progress on the relevant chart, cleaning, washing down, washing up, tidying ropes, polishing brass, cooking, cleaning, working locks, tying up—relaxing, especially on the large commercial waterways, it ain't. So, it was just me and Mick who arrived back at Oudenaarde a few weeks later with a large gallon jar of Sarson's for Marco, ready for the next stage of our little adventure.

We headed north through the huge Oudenaarde Sluis and turned right on to the Ghent Ringvaart towards

Dendermonde. My information on this section was sparse to say the least. Bristow gives the distance from Ghent to Rupelmonde as 67km, and then you're on your own. It was Sunday, a damp and dismal Sunday, and we passed through the enormous 'double effet' sluis at Merelbeke without incident or comment from the keeper way above. The fall was about a foot, and the significance of the double effet had not dawned on me. We were something like 160km from the sea and stupidly I had not realised we were now on the mighty and tidal Zeeschelde.

The tidal bit didn't hit me until I noticed that the bank was passing rapidly by. The GPS showed our speed as almost 12 knots—we were flying. The reduced visibility caused by the persistent misty drizzle combined with our racing speed certainly concentrated the mind. I don't mind tidal rivers, but I do like to be fully prepared and armed at least with a tide table and some idea of the rise and fall. In the event I had neither and the sudden realisation was a bit alarming. We didn't see another vessel in the first 30km to Dendermonde and this didn't exactly help the confidence. By the time we had orientated ourselves with the aid of the odd kilometre post and conspicuous bend, we were speeding past the entrance to the River Dender on our right and shortly afterwards the town of Dendermonde itself loomed at a rate of knots. Mooring on a tidal river is never easy and this was no exception. We hadn't seen a single suitable mooring place since Ghent and the evening, aided and abetted by gloomy weather, was drawing in fast. As we rounded a left-hand bend towards Dendermonde we saw a line of floating pontoons on the left of the river, which turned out to be the base of Dendermonde VVW, the local boat club. This was a relief but first we had to turn in the river and stem the tide. Ahead the wide span of a road bridge before the river disappeared to the right. There was still no traffic and I decided to go for it just downstream of the bridge. The current took us a couple of hundred yards sideways towards the bend before the boat's stem gradually turned into the flow and we progressed very slowly towards the mooring. No sooner had we got a head rope onto the rather flimsy looking cleat, a péniche, pushing into the tide, ploughed into sight around the bend and forged past. Always expect the unexpected!

There was good news and bad news at the VVW. The only day they opened the bar at this time of the year was Sunday, so that was the good news. It also meant that Sunday was the only night they charged for mooring—240 Belgian francs, about £4—a small price to pay for a safe haven, a few beers and some convivial company. One of the members, Luc, took a bit of a shine to Mick. Luc owned a sandwich bar in Aalst on the River Dender. He drew a map and offered us a free lunch if we were going that way. That wasn't the sole reason I decided to change plans and head off up the Dender, to be honest. I didn't really have enough information to carry on any further on the Schelde and the thought of a quieter couple of days proved no contest. As always on these occasions I took the whole folder of official stuff with me—passport, radio licence, international certificate of competence, yacht-masters, ships registration certificate, insurance, proof of ownership—and, as usual, the only thing they were interested in was the ships registration document, called the Small Ships Register (SSR). We were now in Walloon territory and the licence I had bought from Jonah/Johann only covered the Flemish half of Belgium. An official form was completed in sextuplicate and the éclusier carefully split the copies and, referring to a note on the office wall, carefully distributed each one. 'White—that's for the file. Pink—that one goes on the hook. Green—that is yours. Blue—that, er,' he stopped and referred to his notes, 'that goes on this hook. Red—that can go in the bin and yellow, er, that is also yours. And now for the money.' I waited with bated breath as he took out his calculator. After a couple of mis-pressed buttons and a bit of cursing, he announced, '45 francs s'il vous plait.' Forty-five Belgian Francs (we were still in Belgium). That was roughly 65p. For this princely sum we had the attendance of a lock keeper at each of the next ten locks. What is more, I had to take my two copies to each one so they could be inspected, validated and stamped with an almighty thump.

Beer was called for and that night we stayed in the old fortified town of Ath before another 65p worth took us down the 20 locks to the junction with the Canal Nimy a Blaton. Another team of lock keepers followed us over the whole route, and most locks were ready for our arrival. This service, while very welcome, again illustrated the somewhat cramping of style caused by the imposition of the timetable. Each evening we had to inform the team of our departure time the next morning and while 'sept heures s'il vous plait' sounds very impressive the night before, in the event it can be a bit of a liability after a good night ashore.

The wider and much busier Nimy Blaton Canal took us to Mons, where we moored in the Grand Large, a huge lake with another VVW, this time closed and not half as sociable (not a Luc in sight), and three times the price. It crossed my mind to ignore the urgent arm-waving of the harbour master and tie to what looked like a disused wharf, but it was well that I didn't as a very large grain carrier arrived in the small hours and filled the entire space. The centre of Mons was a good half-hour walk but it was well worth the effort and after a stroll around the uneven streets we had an excellent dinner in the Grand Place, where we watched the elegant world of Mons pass by. In 1914 Mons was the site of the first battle undertaken by the British in the First World War. They were forced to retreat by the Germans, who occupied the town for almost four years. The entrance to the city hall bears a plaque which reads: 'Mons was recaptured by the Canadian Corps on the 11th November 1918. After fifty months of German occupation, freedom was restored to the city. Here was fired the last shot of the Great War.'

The following day was one of those red-letter days you get from time to time on a canal voyage, like the first time you go through the Harecastle Tunnel or tackle the Hatton Flight. Our particular landmark was the four boat lifts at Houdeng—four Anderton lifts in the space of a few kilometres that lifted the level of the canal more than 200ft! At times like this you somehow never seem to get there and find yourself anticipating the great event several bends before it actually appears. The morning was dull and overcast, and by the time we did see the 'Meccano No 7' structure ahead in the murky gloom, a stiff breeze had sprung up on our stern. For many years, the Belgian authorities had been construct-ing a massive new single lift to replace the old ones, increasing capacity from 300 to 1,300-ton barges. The project had been severely delayed with financial problems and took 20 years to complete (the final cost was in the region of £400-million), and although the lift itself and the connecting length of canal at the lower end was complete, there was still the upper section to be built; a section that would entail the construction of a vast 5,000m aqueduct. The old lifts were built in 1888 by the British engineer, Edwin Clarke, who was also responsi-ble for the Anderton lift. We were going uphill through the old lifts and the new cathedral-like monolith stood out in the distance. At the point where the new length re-joined the old the entrance into the lock below the first lift, access was through a very narrow arched bridge set at an obtuse angle and the wind was blowing quite strongly on to the starboard quarter.

And that, ladies and gentlemen, is my lame excuse for a pretty naff piece of boatmanship. The wind caught the stern as I turned into the gap. I was going too fast, and the result was one of those painful moments when the boat is trapped at an angle halfway along its length, in this case with the port bow and starboard midships. It twisted itself straight with a sickening crack, which sounded as though the hull had been split wide open like a can of beans. The only other time I'd experienced this was with a narrowboat at the entry to the bottom pair of locks of the Stourport staircase on the Staffs and Worcester Canal. I blamed the wind then, but considering that the working boatmen did it regularly with a loaded 70ft boat (mine was 62ft) and that at Thieu they did it with 38m vessels (mine was 21m), there really wasn't anything to blame but my own stupidity and lack of patience and judgement.

We ascended the first lock and entered the basin below the lift. There was a péniche coming down and it soon became obvious they were only using one caisson. It seemed an age before the light turned to green and we were finally on our way into the huge tank of No 4 lift. The first three lifts we ascended without incident, the ancient mechanism squeaking and grinding as slowly but surely, we rose the 60ft or so to the next level. The longest pound came between the third and fourth lift and though we had a green light, nothing seemed to be happening. It was 4.45pm and we waited for more than half an hour before resigning ourselves to the fact that the lift was closed, even though my information stated 5pm. We were in the middle of nowhere and had to make do with a fry-up with what little provisions we had on board. Mick managed a very edible sausage cakes, eggs, chips and beans, which went down rather well with a couple of beers.

The next morning, we were ready at 8am but although the light still showed green there was no evident movement until we noticed that the top caisson moving. Another commercial was coming down. We watched as the caisson faltered and stopped, moved a few more feet, stopped again, started again, shuddered a bit, faltered and stopped. Men appeared at various points with large buckets and painted the running gear with a black oily gunge. The caisson moved a few more feet and groaned and whined until it finally came to a stop at the bottom. The guillotine gate rose up and a 38m loaded péniche motored slowly out beneath a cascade of water pouring from the massive gate, passing us with a friendly wave that seemed to say, 'best of luck mate.'

A few months later we read of a disaster in this very same lift when the hydraulic ram failed and started rising beneath a laden péniche just as it was leaving the caisson. The boat split in two and was sent headlong through the half-raised gate, smashing its wheelhouse. Miraculously nobody was seriously hurt. It spelt the end of the Houdeng lifts; they were listed and were awaiting funding to be fully restored. It also meant that work on completing the new lift at Strepy Thieu took on a renewed urgency. Had we known about it in advance, we might have thought twice about entering this imminent death trap, but ignorance is bliss. We finally got to the top after a lot of sticking-plaster type attention, our faltering progress interrupted by frequent stops and lashings of grease slapped on with a stick, frowns and frenzied discussion from the ascenseurs. At the top the guillotine rose up and led us into a further trough with yet another guillotine gate leading back into the canal itself. After several minutes of coaxing it became obvious that the gate was not going to move, and we were told to tie up and wait. The sun came out, so we made some coffee and bathed in the warmth on top of the world, oblivious of the 80ft drop beneath us. An evidently technical sort of bloke arrived in the white Renault van and an impressive box of tools. After about 90 minutes, the gate was persuaded to rise, and we were on our way again.

The intention was to head for Charleroi for the night, a town I had driven though some years before and which seemed pleasant enough. But Mrs Bradshaw was not very encouraging ('no satisfactory mooring giving access to city—possible to tie to concrete posts supporting roadway below écluse but athletic crew required for this!' she declared). As a result of some not very clever planning, however, rather than any doubts about our athleticism, I mistook Charleroi itself for the Hades that confronted us at the junction of the River Sambre at Montignies. Here we entered into Dante's Inferno (I'm talking about the actual Dante's Inferno here): the sky turned yellowy-black with the fumes of a thousand belching chimneys, dimly lit doorways revealing blazing orange furnaces and crackling sparks of arc welders which now and then illuminated an alien ghost-like goggle-faced figure clad in dirty-white asbestos overalls. Lines of rusty brown ballast wagons stood in sidings alongside mountains of iron slag and the noise of hammering and escaping steam made conversation impossible. It was as dark as night, and on the spur of the moment I decided to turn south on to the Sambre and leave Charleroi for another day.

This was the Black Country of Belgium and the largest industrial area: glassworks, coal mines and steel manufac-turing all seemingly concentrated around the canal. Just a few kilometres further on, hell gave way, incredibly, to a lush green winding river valley and peace and quiet once more. The silence was almost deafening, broken now and again by a suburban rattler on the railway line alongside. By the time we arrived at the lock at Landelies, it was past closing time and the only possible place to moor was against the dolphins below the lock. It wasn't ideal but we had no choice. I checked to ensure that we weren't blocking the entrance to the lock, although I really didn't expect any traffic.

Once again... expect the unexpected! At 7am next morning we felt a gentle swell and a 38m slid past with inches to spare and nosed into the lock. There was nothing much at Landelies, a small hamlet at the top of a steep narrow lane, apart from the annual fair. They seemed to be putting one on just for us wherever we went. A little bar, bustling with locals, did not provide food but had no objection to people bringing in burgers and frites acquired from a stall next to the dodgems, topped-up with mountains of mayonnaise, to be washed down with a glass of strong local Witte (wheat, or white) beer. I had grown to like this refreshing drink and especially a particular Dutch brew called Hoegaarden, with a slice of lime. When in Rome, take your burger and chips into the bar, so that's what we did.

After an extremely pleasant few hours cruising on this delightful stretch of river, not unlike some of the tree-lined reaches of the Thames in places, we arrived at Thuin, a 'pleasant barge town' according to Mrs B, where many retired bateliers had chosen to drop their proverbial hook and retire. The town was split on two levels, the larger part high above the canal. There was also a busy barge shipyard with slipways and docking facilities. We found a space to tie right on the quay. My original plan was to continue south into France and a winter mooring, possibly at St Symphorien. There was a small yard there run by an English canal exile, Roger Wolster.

The canal maintenance programme in France differed from Britain in that it operated throughout the year. BW shut complete canals during the winter but only worked on emergency repairs in the summer season. The English canals were virtually totally dominated by leisure boating, so the theory was that this system caused the least disruption. It doesn't please everyone, of course, such as private boat owners who like to move all year round and who had, after all, paid for an annual licence, would get somewhat pissed off to be told they couldn't use an entire length of canal for three months just because one lock had to be de-gated.

The French had a different system. The stoppages are scattered randomly throughout the year. These closures (or chomages) were published annually in a list I'd got from the French tourism office in London. It was printed in a miniscule type and quite frankly I'd not paid a great deal of attention to it until now. As we were actually in France, I thought it might be an idea to at least have a look at it. It took about half an hour to decipher and arrive at the conclusion there were several closures that would certainly affect us unless we got a serious move on.

Chapter 8

Northern France
and the Schelde

W E HEADED south from Thuin and entered France at Jeumont unnoticed. Here we stocked up with amazingly cheap wine and beer at a canal-side Lidl and changed our Belgian francs for French. We took down our Belgian courtesy flag and replaced it with a French one. The flags of Holland, Belgium, France and Germany were a bit confusing and I tried to work out an aide-memoire to help get the correct one and avoid upsetting the indigenous population. The French and Dutch were both red, white and blue. I managed to think of these as laid-back Dutch horizontal stripes, which left the vertical variety for the French. Applying this theory to the Belgian and German flags left me more confused. They were both red, yellow and black but the laid-back approach rather fell on its face as the horizontal one belonged not to the Belgians, but the Germans.

At the first French écluse, at Marpent, I had to present the papiers again and finally get legal with a French permis (I never did get one at Dunkirk!). These were issued on several different bases and the most convenient seemed to be a 30-day licence. This allowed for 30 actual cruising days. You got a card with squares on it and you are trusted to mark in each date that you are on the move. We were also given a magic box called Sesame that ingeniously prepared and operated locks for us at the touch of a button. There was a set of instructions in English, the last of these being a touching 'please do not drop me into the water as I cannot swim.' As we approached the radio antenna before each lock, Sesame would bleep, and the messages were somewhat suggestive! 'I am getting ready for you' or 'please come closer' would appear on the screen and then 'goodbye' as we left the lock. This worked extremely well, and we passed through Mauberge, Hautmont, Aulnoye–Aymeries, Berlaimont and Landrecies with the urgency of one on a mission.

The last lock under Sesame rule was at Bois L'Ab-baye. We were now on the summit level and here we handed back our little friend and stopped for the night. So far so good; we were making progress. I had noticed a slight knock from the engine as I engaged the gear for the past few days but hadn't paid much attention to it. That evening I was down in the engine room getting out my wet gear before we tied up and as Mick put the engine into reverse, I noticed that the gearbox moved a good inch independently of the engine. When we'd tied up, I had another look and found I could move the whole gearbox quite freely. This seemed like very bad news.

Now we were in France, I was using the Carte Guides charts, the French linear cruising guides, and this mentioned a boat repairer in Landrecies which we had passed about five or six kilometres back. My knowledge of mechanical things was about on a par with my carpentry and this was definitely out of my range. I called the number shown in the guide and a wiry, intense Frenchman with about as much English as my French turned up in a van an hour or so later and began poking and pushing and shaking his head pessimistically. I couldn't work out whether he was appraising the job or adding up the francs he could charge. He managed to communicate there was nothing he could do on the spot and that we must gently return to his workshop. This was situated above the lock at Landrecies, so we turned around and gingerly retraced our steps. There was a converted 38m péniche in the layby at Landrecies, and I turned Saul Trader under the watchful gaze of the batelier, tying up alongside the small yard hopeful of a quick repair. This was not to be. I was reminded of the old sailor's superstition of never predicting anything, least of all an arrival time after a long passage.

Spanners, as the Frenchman became known to us, named after the sign over his premises, told me sadly that the job was far too big for him and our only chance was to return to the shipyard at Thuin. This sounded like a time-consuming and expensive exercise and I wondered what the hell to do next. I didn't want to risk doing more damage by going any further. Our neighbour, the batelier, was another Luc, a Dutchman who could have passed for Mike Harding, and who, with his partner Jentine, spent six months of every year aboard their converted 38m barge Reve, working an antique stall in the indoor market at Liege during the winter. We spent a very sociable evening in their wheelhouse. 'I weel be shailing at 8 in the morning and so then you can come into theese place,' said Luc. It was 2.30am!

It was more than 12 hours later that we finally waved goodbye to them; more wine had been consumed than initially anticipated! I had a word with the friendly éclusier, Francisse, whose house was alongside the lock. It was nearly October and it was looking less and less likely that we would ever get the repair completed in time. Francisse spoke to his boss and confirmed we could stay there until the new year. He told me there would be no charge made by the VNF, but we could make a donation at the Mairie to a fund for homeless children. There was water and electricity and a good mooring on a floating pontoon. I also knew that Francisse would keep an eye on the boat while I decided what to do.

The next day another English boat arrived, a former Leeds & Liverpool short boat, the Nidd, with Paul and Sally, who also arranged to stay for the winter. Paul kindly offered to have a look at the gearbox and came to the same conclusion as Spanners. The whole box needed to be moved back from the engine far enough to allow someone to get a hand in the gap to retrieve and re-tighten the bolts that held the bell housing, and this was going to be extremely difficult in the necessarily confined space. I really didn't like the idea of leaving the boat for the winter without the work on the gearbox being sorted out so I spoke to Phil Trotter, who seemed to think it could be done—but he was 300 miles away! Nothing phased my practical brother and a dozen packs of Golden Virginia persuaded him to come over and have a go at it. I drove to Oostende to pick him up from the SeaCat. His bag was full of tools and weighed a ton; I thought the ferry Captain must have asked him to stand in the middle of the ship! The foot passengers' ramp was about half a mile long and he eventually appeared, groaning and straining under the weight.

To the amazement of Spanners and Paul, Roy had the job sewn up within a couple of hours, once he had actually started it. The mental preparation and planning had taken a couple of days, but that's my brother—everything has to be just right. He would study the job for hours, continuously muttering how he couldn't do it. I would leave him to it and half an hour later look in to find him squatting over the engine, spanner in hand, humming tunelessly. This was a good sign; once he was humming, the job was going fine. We stayed in Landrecies for a few more days and Roy did some more small jobs that had been on my must-do-urgently list for about six months. The town was fairly quiet and had virtually shut down for the winter. The bars and few restaurants seemed to share the evenings of the week between them so that not more than one or two were ever open at the same time. We entertained and were entertained by Paul and Sally, telling stories of our various adventures. The Nidd had crossed the Channel from Boston and had bumbled, as Paul put it, slowly through the canals of northern France. They seemed quite content to cruise for three or four hours and then tie up for a couple of weeks—not quite my cup of tea, but they had made many friends among the locals and Paul had picked up a very passable knowledge of French. He told me about a cheap way to make phone calls on the mobile. During the first couple of months my bill had been horrendous, at nearly £400 a month. I used it for connecting to the internet and for making and (just as expensively) receiving calls from the UK. I was being charged £1 per minute for calls to the UK (another example of the Great British Rip-Off). Following Paul's advice, I purchased a French pay-as-you-go sim card for about £15, which immediately reduced the charge to the UK to 60p per minute. I then subscribed to an American service which meant having to dial a number in the US, hanging up after the first ring, waiting a few seconds for a call back, and on hearing a sweet South Carolina drawl say 'Americom', I could then ring the UK, using a code as if I was phoning from the States, for an unbelievable 11p per minute—crazy or what! It worked and my monthly bills were reduced to the usual £60-£70 and about 10 or 12 dollars for Americom. I couldn't work out how to use this system to access the internet, but I got wise and used an internet café whenever I could. Subsequently I purchased Dutch and Belgian sim cards. The only problem was remembering all the numbers and codes and remembering which cards were in which phones! Nowadays of course there are many ways of keeping in touch. It's all too much for me; I couldn't get over an American I once came across lost on the Ashby Canal in a narrowboat using GPS!

Spanners was a constant source of amusement. Apart from the small boat repairs, Paul said he was a plongeur—not what I first thought it meant! Apparently, he was also a diving instructor. Business was obviously not very brisk during the winter and he had optimistically stocked some four-wheeled all terrain bikes. He kept them in a garage at the side of his workshop and roared them out each morning to line them up against the wall. Several times a day he'd jump onto one and race around the forecourt, standing up in the saddle like Evil Knievel. He seemed to particularly like to do this at the times young women were passing by on their way to and from the school. One day he was so transfixed by one of these young ladies (who, incidentally, hadn't seemed to notice him at all) that he leapt on Wild West style, kick-started the bike in the standing position, flicked the bike into gear and drove it flat out—straight into a wall. As you can probably tell, there wasn't much in the way of entertainment in Landrecies. When we had finally shut the boat down and put the winter covers on the wheelhouse, we returned to England happy in the knowledge that there would always be someone around to keep an eye on it.

As it happened, it was just as well. In the middle of February, I got a call from Paul to say Saul Trader had developed a list. They'd had a couple of weeks of freezing weather and it seemed as though something had burst during the thaw. It was another reminder that Saul Trader was the boss and if I didn't get my act together, I'd get a gentle (or maybe not so gentle) reminder. The two forward domestic water tanks each had separate shut-off valves. I had noticed that one of the gate valves had not been shutting off fully; another thing I'd been meaning to look at one day. So, I paid the price and had to make an unscheduled trip to France.

I found that a simple acorn coupling in the plastic plumbing connecting the water tank to the pump had pulled apart with the frost and emptied all the contents of the fresh water into the engine room. The teco board we used as a deck covering in the engine room was awash, and the water had risen above the prop shaft guide and flooded the back cabin bilge to within a couple of inches of the floor. It could have been worse. The central heating burst into life at the first attempt and the boat soon got warm, so much so that I was able to decline Paul's kind offer of a berth aboard Nidd. As the water was contaminated with oil and sludge from the engine bilge, I had to get the Pompiers in to pump it out. Once that was done, conditions soon returned to normal. In the time-honoured tradition of stable doors and bolting horses, I then set about curing the problem. I managed to get the offending valve out of its highly inaccessible hole and Paul came with me as interpreter to get a replacement. Another (expensive) lesson learnt.

It was Easter when Mick, Scragg and I returned. Scragg had worked out he could have more than ten days off but only lose four days of actual holiday leave. I had started to use Norfolk Line for the Channel crossing, which sailed to Dunkirk. In those days most of the passengers were lorry drivers. The restaurant on Midnight Merchant was a floating transport café where you could pass off as a lorry driver and get a very good fry-up for about three quid. There was usually plenty of space, which meant you could stretch out and get a bit of kip on the two-hour crossing. For some reason though, they insisted on showing videos in one corner of the lounge. It was always some disaster movie, an earthquake-in-Chicago sort of thing. I suppose they thought it would appeal to the average lorry driver. The result was I would get 15 minutes or so when nothing would happen and just as I was lulled into a hazy sleep, skyscrapers would collapse and explode, and screams, shouts and fire truck sirens would wake me up in shaking terror. I complained to the purser about it once. 'Couldn't you show something a bit less dramatic during the night, like Bambie or something?' He laughed and said they only actually carried the one video.

When we got back to the boat, we found it sitting nicely on an even keel. We had been away for more than two months and yet it always surprised me how quickly the boat regained a lived-in feel. Once the heating circulated a bit of hot water, it was as though we'd never been away. Saul Trader was spray-foam insulated, and I always left the quarter-light windows and connecting doors open. This seemed to minimise condensation and we rarely had any problems. I'd changed my mind about going south. Paul had convinced me to put off the temptation of the Med until we'd had a chance to fully explore the north and central France, so we decided to go to Holland instead.

I'd heard about a festival called Dordt in Stoom, a weekend of steam (boats, trains and vintage transport) that took place in Dordrecht in May. It was always nice to have a goal. We could have gone by several different routes but I opted to travel south on the Sambre, turn right at the bottom and follow the Canal St Quentin through Cambrai and into Belgium, then traverse the boat lifts again before continuing through Charleroi and

Namur on the Meuse and so through Maastricht into Holland.

But... best laid plans and all that! Unfortunately, the top lift at Houdeng had been badly damaged in the nasty accident and the general consensus was there was no way it was going to re-open for some time. In fact, it had prompted the Belgian authorities to get on and finish the new lift and this was obviously taking priority. The rumour was it would be open to traffic in the middle of the summer but in the event, the first boats did not pass through until late September. So, we had to change our plans, and this meant returning to Ghent, taking the dreaded Schelde to Antwerp, and then into Holland via the Willemsvaart Canal. Before we left Landrecies, I gave Francisse and his wife Martine a couple of bottles of Pastis and some chocolates—and an English Inland Waterways Calendar—in appreciation of their hospitality. Francisse had lived and worked on the canal all his life and was very interested in its history, and he'd shown us his collection of historic photographs. He was passionately devoted to his job and once told me sadly how he frowned upon the rest of the gang who disappeared to the bar each lunchtime for a two-hour break. I don't think he quite came to terms with the miserable little things we call canal boats, but they told us we'd be welcome at any time and frantically waved us out of sight like old friends.

The passage over the summit of the Sambre and down to the junction with the Canal de Saint-Quentin was made in indifferent weather which somehow matched the environment. We had the assistance of the éclusiers all the way, even though at some locks we didn't even see them. The gates would be ready and open and once secured with a back line, we raised a rod alongside the lock and sat back and watched while we were gently lowered, and the bottom gates creaked open. At Fargniers we turned right into the Canal de Saint-Quentin. The locks were all doubled at some time, although only one was now used, and which one varied from lock to lock. The Carte Guide, once I had it orientated, indicated which side was in use and was (usually) correct. After the first three locks at Terniers we moored in darkness at a little town called Quessy. The only sign of life came from the massive goods yard that lay alongside the canal. All night long trains arrived and were shunted via a hump into 60 or more sidings, shunters running alongside with poles and chocks to stop the runaway wagons. There was a footbridge that spanned the entire yard. I could have stayed and watched all night, but it was too bloody cold!

The tunnel at Saint-Quentin was 6km long and passage was by a convoy of electric tugs taking current from overhead wires. At the approach to the Requeval tunnel bollards lined both sides of the canal for about 5km indicating some pretty dense use. This was obviously all in the past as there were just two commercials waiting at the entrance when we arrived. The tunnel keeper wrote down some details of Saul Trader from the registration document, and we threw a line to the second barge and were away. The bore is as large as a railway tunnel and is brightly lit throughout its length. The passage takes two hours, so it doesn't take much to work out that the speed is about 3km (two miles) per hour. Being the tail-end Charlie meant that we swung a bit from side to side but there was hardly any need to steer. Wooden guards along both sides ensured that the roof of the wheelhouse, although sometimes coming uncomfortably close, never touched the brickwork. Nobody asked for money and eventually we emerged into daylight. The batelier in front threw back our line and we were on our own again. We went into a little disused harbour at Vendhuile for the night. The tiny village was absolutely deserted; everything was closed and hardly a light twinkled behind the tightly closed shutters. Maybe they had heard about Mick and were protecting their daughters!

The next day we got to Cambrai, the base of a close-knit group of members of the Dutch Barge Association (DBA). They'd formed the Continental Cruising Group, providing, mostly through Tam & Di Murrell on their barge Friesland, a lot of very useful information for anyone 'going foreign'. They also produced an instructional video from which Malcolm had learned his lassoing skills and ran courses for the French Permis de Plaisance certificate, required for skippers of vessels in excess of 24m in length. They moored in the harbour at Cambrai, (Paul called it Heroes Harbour), and not being much of a clubber myself, probably because I am just plain antisocial, I had decided to tie in a disused arm some way past the harbour. Paul had told me about the dead arm and there was just enough room for Saul Trader to turn and tie up close to the end. I did go over to the harbour as I would like to have met Tam and Di, but there was no sign of them. We had a lunchtime drink in the bar and were entertained by an Italian spiv selling novelties from a suitcase. Mick bought a magnetic stick for five Euros which he seemed to think might come in useful, although how and when I must say escaped me. I also managed, with no very great difficulty, to avoid buying a sort of maniacal mechanical mouse that zoomed around the floor, giving everyone a great laugh in driving the pub cat to distraction. We were now of course in Euros, and what a joy. Being able to use the same currency in France, Belgium and Holland made things so much easier.

Cambrai was a textile town boasting a strange combination of food specialities: chitterlings and mints. Apparently, the Battle of Cambrai during the First World War had the dubious honour to be the first to use tanks. Maybe that's why it was twinned with Gravesend! There was another typically French square and we soon found a convenient bar, Le Bureau, where we could eat well, drink Guinness on a mortgage and watch busy barmaids dancing around to bluesy music while they worked. The Bureaux was in fact part of a chain and we found them all over France, a bit like the British Wetherspoons; no frills but decent food and good service.

North of Cambrai the Canal de Saint-Quentin becomes the Escaut, which in turn becomes the Schelde, and we followed this river all the way to Antwerp. The locks were doubled all the way to Fresnes sur L'Escaut and all manned by éclusiers. At one I was asked for my permis; inadvertently I'd forgotten to mark in the day. Mon dieu, would it mean the Bastille, or deportation! As it happened the éclusiers merely glanced at it, smiled and handed it back with a polite 'merci, monsieur'. We turned left at the junction as I wanted to take on fuel at the bunker station at Antoing. As it was a Sunday and the fuelling station was closed, we carried on to Tournai for the night. Here I made another faux pas. In attempting to get close to the town and avoid tying to a rather steep wall, I passed a red light. Commercial traffic generally rested up on Sundays and we hadn't seen anything else on the move. Beyond the light the channel narrowed down quite dramatically to one boat width with walls on each side, and the flow increased accordingly. A sharp bend and then a lift bridge, in the closed position—red light on. Nowhere to tie and much too narrow anyway. I had to make an embarrassing exit backwards, watched by what seemed the entire population of Tournai out for a Sunday afternoon promenade, and probably thinking, with some justification, that we were a bunch of bloody English imbeciles!

Luckily Saul Trader behaved itself impeccably and reversed in a perfect straight line. Minutes after we were secured safely to the wall, two 1,000-tonners appeared edging through the tight channel and tied up quietly behind us side by side. Uncanny isn't it! Tournai, the oldest town in Belgium, was an absolutely lovely place. By the time we went ashore it was dusk and the town was floodlit in a most spectacularly atmospheric way. Blues music emanated from a canal-side bar and the Grand Place, dominated by the magnificent cathedral with its five square domes, was alive with illuminated dancing fountains, and surrounded with subtly floodlit buildings rich in a variety of architectural styles. I was completely captivated by the place and wondered why it didn't feature on the front pages of all the tour operators' brochures. It was a well-preserved secret, free from the ice cream waving hordes that marred the likes of Bruges—and hopefully always will be. We found a little café and took in the atmosphere before returning by a roundabout route that led past the ramparts of the old fortifications straddling the canal, to the blues bar that by now was heaving and swaying to the music.

Monday morning was alive with canal traffic again; the commercials started to move at 6am after their day off. We returned to Antoing to top up with cheaper tax-free red diesel which in those days was available in Belgium but not France. The fuel station was a large floating pontoon and provided several tanker barges that supplied the commercials with a RAS (Re-fuel At Sea), on the move. A call on the radio and the little tankers ploughed off to rendezvous with their customer, nestling alongside as they discharged their load at a prodigious rate and the commercial hardly reducing speed, before casting off and sending the replenished giant steaming on its way again. We took 1,200 litres and against my better judgement I was persuaded not to use my own filter as it would seriously slow the filling process, and anyway the pump had its own filter built in, according to the gadgee. I worried about the purity of red diesel and about the capacity of my filter system to deal with it. However, I paid up—about the same as the price on the UK canals at the time, 45 Euros (30p) per litre—and we were on our way.

At Berchem's Kerkove Sluis, I had to buy another Flemish licence to cover the next six months to June. We stopped in Oudenaarde again and this time stayed against the wall in the main canal. I put out a couple of springs and a good spread of fenders and we rode quite comfortably in the considerable swell. The big commercials were still playing chicken with the bridge opening and the bar was still full of complaining market traders. In Ghent I decided to go into the centre by a different route. The Navicarte showed the Kanaal Ghent-Ostende to be navigable and we followed the Ringvaart to the entrance. I turned in, keeping well outside the corner, and right on the apex of the turn, at no speed at all, we stuck fast. No amount of reverse or bow thruster would shift us. The bottom was a thick sludge of silt and we were firmly embedded in it. The junction here was a crossroad, and a very busy one as it turned out: to the left was the canal from Ostende and ahead the sluis at Evergem and the busy sea canal to Terneuzen.

I thought the wash from these commercials as they swept by to join the Ringvaart might be enough to lift us clear, but there was nothing doing. It was getting towards late afternoon and starting to get a bit worrying. We tried dropping the anchor with the dinghy and dragging ourselves off with a kedge but that was hopeless. We tried pulling the bow off with a line attached to the dinghy but the only effect of that was Scragg being flung around in the rubber boat like a Wurlitzer at a fair, to the amusement of everyone except Scragg. It reminded me of an old fisherman, Biddy the Tubman, who used to perform off the beach at Hastings when I was young, rolling round and round in his barrel in the surf. Still we didn't budge an inch. There was only one option left: we would have to swallow our pride and ask one of the commercials for assistance. A large container-laden ship was passing to enter the sluis. I communicated our predicament with the international code of sign language: a combination of the cradle motion you do at Twickenham during Swing Low Sweet Chariot to indicate the bottom, combined with a simulated cutting of the throat to indicate 'I'm in schtook.' He understood immediately and agreed to take a line—the power of Esperanto!

Scragg scooted across in the dinghy and the line was attached to his stern, and with a thrust of his prop and a spin of the wheel, we slowly slid free. We thanked him in the time-honoured way of a bottle of wine (we only had good stuff left) and he told us that the canal I had intended using was closed. My chart was obviously out of date again. Nautical charts can be regularly updated from Correction Notices and it was the job of the junior deck officers to perform this arduous task, carefully marking the charts in pencil where buoys had been moved or where light characteristics had been changed and so on. No such luxury, or should that read drudgery, was afforded to inland navigators! The only viable alternative was to retrace our course along the Ringvaart and go into the city the same way as before.

There was no gesticulator this time, and space on the pontoon adjacent to the yacht club made for perfect (and free) mooring! 'We don't go far,' said Mick philosophically, 'but we do see life!' Scragg and I went off for a tour of the inner canals in the dinghy and we soon found the barrier to our approach from the other route—a disused lock. Ghent was a major industrial city and connected to the North Sea some 20 miles away by the Terneuzen Canal. The canal had been enlarged and modernised over the years and could now be used by vessels of up 125,000 tons with a draft of 12.5m. It was 200m wide and handled some 45 million tons per year. As a result, Ghent was a major logistical centre for northern Europe, distributing freight by inland waterway, rail and road. The largest boat that can access the centre of Birmingham can carry 25 tons at a push! We managed to leave Ghent by a different route—one that was shown as impassable on my chart! I suppose that's what exploring canals is all about. I don't want to know exactly what's round the next corner until I get there. I can understand the need for a bit of planning but why take away the adventure? It reminded me of my old man who'd write to the AA to get a printed route to take us in his old Ford Pop sit-up-and-beggar to Cornwall for our holidays. I wonder what he'd have made of a built-in sat nav!

The back-double brought us via the Muinkshelde Canal into the Ringvaart at Merelbeke Sluis, and the River Scheldt. I wasn't going to be caught out this time and made my way to the office for a tide table. They looked at me strangely and I got the distinct impression I was probably the first person who'd ever asked for such a thing. Finally, a nice lady brought me a piece of paper with some numbers scribbled on the back. 'It is very small change,' she assured me, 'it will not be a problem for you.' Oh well—I did ask.

In front of us a 1,000-tonner, loaded to the side decks, churned slowly out of the lock. In the narrow channel there was no room to pass and I patiently waited to overtake. No chance! As soon as he'd cleared the channel and got into deeper water he was away in a cloud of smoke, never to be seen again. From Ghent to Antwerp it was

88km and then a further 80 or so to the North Sea. We left Merelbeke Lock at 10am. My piece of paper showed we would be pushing the tide for an hour or so and have the benefit of the flow behind us for most of the way to Antwerp. I saw this as a mixed blessing. It meant we would be dicing with the heavy shipping in Antwerp with a three or four knot current behind us. I was always wary when running with the current and reading about the port in Bristow did not afford much comfort: 16,000 ships a year, 30 miles of quays and 3,500 acres of port installation. Neither did Mrs Bradshaw's advice of 'very shallow on bends—follow a loaded péniche if you can.' We couldn't; they were much too fast, and several overtook us, ploughing past flat out with a raised hand from the steerer, like waterborne juggernauts, causing us to dive down into their vortex as though on a waterslide. As usual in these situations, however, the word proved much worse than the deed!

Where the shoals were most prevalent, around Hoboken, a busy industrial town with vast shipyards lining both banks, the channel was clearly marked with buoys. The multitude of ships never materialised either, probably due to the tidal state. We passed a couple of ocean-going tugs but very few commercial barges, and it was almost with a sense of anti-climax that we approached Antwerp. We'd made pretty good time since the turn of the tide and by 3pm we could make out the handsome buildings lining the waterfront and the hulks of ancient vessels on display in the Maritime Museum. Eventually we picked out the entrance to Royers Sluice, our landfall and the gateway to the inner harbour. As we turned into the holding dock the huge gate was sliding shut behind a crane barge and we tied to the staithes to wait. There we sat and waited. And waited. Slowly the crane on its floating pontoon was raised skywards. I broke a golden rule and we had a glass of wine. After an hour we were still there, and nothing seemed to be happening. Scragg climbed the rusty ladder to survey the situation, and a man appeared from the lock-side waving and shouting. 'You must go out,' he shouted down, cupping his hands to his mouth. 'Why—what's the problem?' 'You must radio to the lock for coming inside.' 'OK—I'll do that from here.' 'No—you must go out to the seaway and speak to the radio.'

I thought this was a bit bloody-minded but stopped myself from telling him so—just as well, as it happened. 'We have eight barges before you that will come inside and first you must speak on the radio.' Eight barges—where? I really thought he was taking the mickey. However, we were in no position to argue so I cast off and turned Saul Trader back into the tideway, back towards Ghent. There on the wall was a line of thousand tonners, one behind the other. Where the hell had they come from? As we motored slowly past, the leading one started to move towards the lock. One by one, the other seven joined the procession. I turned around to tag on to the back of the queue and spoke to the lock. 'We are 21 metres only,' I pleaded, feeling stupid at trying to speak English in the same way as them.

Scragg asked me once whether Saul Trader was pronounced differently in French. 'Of course not,' I said, 'why do you ask?' 'Because you always say it with a French accent—Saul Trradeur.' Good point. Shades of the infamous interview with Steve McClaren after he had taken over as manager of the Dutch side FC Twente. They were due to play Arsenal in the Champions League and when asked about their chances by a Radio 5 presenter, said 'Ven ve play ze Ars–en–al ve vill play our normal game and ve are happy ve can vin zis match!'

'Largeur?' barked the radio. 'Four metres.' One by one the giant leviathans disappeared into the lock. How big was it, for God's sake! The radio crackled again, and I couldn't make out what they were saying. 'He's calling us,' said Scragg, 'he said Eengleesh Trradeur.' That was good enough. I opened the throttle and turned around. The lock had swallowed up all eight barges and we sheepishly crept in behind, half expecting another barked instruction from the lock keeper. A friendly batelier took our ropes and we squeezed into the middle, three out from the wall. As soon as we settled, the massive gates slid shut. Then a voice called down from on high. 'Papiers s'il vous plait monsieur.' OK—how did I get up? The skipper of the next-door barge waved me across his stern with a smile. I crossed over the sterns of the two commercials and realised the ladder was too far astern for me to reach it. 'Moment.' said the skipper of the innermost barge, and with a roar he put his engine into reverse and moved the whole entourage 20ft astern to line me up with the ladder. 'No good to swim today,' the skipper laughed, 'it's too early.' And too bloody cold no doubt, I muttered as I clambered up, papiers firmly held between my teeth.

The lock keeper was amazingly friendly in spite of the debacle, no doubt used to the stupid Eenglissh. He gave me an FM number which, if I quoted on any subsequent visit to Antwerp, would alleviate all the paperwork. 'Too much always these papersh,' he said, casting an eye over the bank of radar screens silently surveying the entire area of the lock and river approaches. He must have seen us coming about two hours ago! 'Itsh no problem,' he added, in response to my pathetic apologies for being a prat and trying to jump the queue.

Once inside the dock, the next thing was to find the basin I'd been recommended to use. Traffic moved in all directions, and we kept out of the way. I had a small plan of the layout on the back of the Belgian Carte Guide, but it wasn't particularly clear. We were heading for Kempish Dock. All the bridges were manned and had names. The problem was that the names weren't shown on the actual bridges! We passed through Siberia Brug only to find the one connecting with Kempish Dock was closed. This meant we had to request a second passage of Siberia Brug and hold up more road traffic. We would soon be getting a reputation. Everyone was pleasant enough, but I couldn't help thinking that us pleasure boaters must be a bloody pain in a place like this, teeming with commercialism and quiet efficiency. Or perhaps they saw us as a mildly amusing diversion. Waterloo Brug brought us eventually to the far side of Kempish Dock and a quiet mooring within striking distance of the city.

We did the Maritime Museum and the tourist bus tour, always a good way to orientate yourself in a strange city. There were a number of ship's chandlers near the dock and we bought 20 litres of tar varnish for 22 Euros. The assistant told us if we wanted to tar the boat in the water, now was the time to do it. 'In Belgium everything is allowed. If you get caught doing it in Holland, they put you in jail.' So Scragg spent the following afternoon in the dinghy doing it, and we were careful not to spill any in the dock despite the advice. I went by train to Cambrai to collect the car. The central station in Antwerp has been judged by some as the greatest example of railway architecture in the world. The exterior approach presented a striking façade that looked more like a great cathedral, topped with a huge dome. The interior of the booking hall, which was constructed in iron and glass, covering 12,000 square metres and was quite breath-taking with its marble floor and high vaulted ceiling. The station was essentially a terminus but at the time was in the middle of a massive 1.6-billion Euro reconstruction to create an underground bypass tunnel with two platforms connecting with Berchem station to alleviate the need for high-speed through trains to reverse. The project began in 1998 and wasn't finished until 2007. I think the work was further complicated by the fact that some of the foundations had been disturbed during German bombing in the Second World War.

We left Saul Trader in Antwerp for five weeks. There was a guy moored next to us on a Dutch Tjalk who said he'd keep an eye on the boat and I gave him my phone number. When we returned, he was gone but the boat had come to no harm. This time it was just me and Mick.

Chapter 9

Holland and Dordt in Stoom

I T AMAZED me that I was not charged for that stay in
Antwerp. They had my name and address at the port
control but somehow, I escaped a bill. We threaded
our way through the Saturday-quiet docks and out on
to the Albert Canal. We passed one large vessel that
threw us around alarmingly in its wash and then, all was
calm. I wanted to go via the Dessel-Turnhout Canal, but
the first lock was obviously closed for the day and as
it was still early, we decided to keep going. We passed
through Wijnegem Lock and then, three kilometres
further, the engine faltered, coughed a couple of times
and stopped. There was a small commercial heading up
to Antwerp and I let him pass before slowly bouncing
and bumping with the aid of the bow thruster towards
the concrete wall, where Mick jumped ashore with a

line. It's no good trying to stop Saul Trader by hand.

Mick walked along with the line until most of the weigh had come off and we could tie up properly. The bollards were much too far apart on these commercial canals for us to get two lines on but fortunately there was a stumpy concrete post conveniently placed to take the stern rope. I tried the starter several more times, but it was having none of it. I sat in the engine room cursing and swearing at it but still it didn't respond. My answer to most problems of this nature is to have a cup of coffee. I was sitting in the wheelhouse contemplating our fate when I saw a little white van bombing towards us in a cloud of dust. I know, I know, we can't moor here… busy commercial canal etc, etc. But it wasn't that at all. The officer merely came to tell us that the canal just ahead of us at Viersel would be closed from 10am to 4pm the following day for a power boat race. It looked as though we were going to be stuck for the weekend. Willy came in for a coffee. He had worked for the waterway authority for 18 years. He loved the job, the freedom and environment, and he was obviously proud of his country's superb inland waterway system. We decided it must be the filter blocked again and I set to dismantling the lift pump. Sure enough, the little gauze filter—the same one that had failed back at Devizes—was blocked solid with black sediment. Once this was cleaned and the pump reconnected, the engine burst into life.

It was too late to move on. The evening was settling in, so we decided to do the same. We had plenty of stores aboard and I set about cooking a great pot of chilli con carne which we washed down with a couple of bottles of red and damn the expense. The following day, intrigued by the roar of a hundred powerful outboard engines, we took a stroll along the towpath to watch what turned out to be the Belgian round of the international water-skiing Grand Prix. Hundreds of spectators lined the banks and bridges. Britain was represented by a couple of skiers who, in the time-honoured tradition, did very well, tried extremely hard against all the odds and were a little unlucky, but inevitably got beaten… by the bloody Aussies! When it had finished, the water subsided to a ripple and the motorhomes and campers started to file out of the circuit. Saul Trader steamed slowly down the course like a VIP launch at a boat race, and a few of the British spectators saluted the ensign with a cheeky wave. That evening we moored on the pontoon below Herentals Lock, where the Bocholt Canal branched off towards the Netherlands. It was a Sunday, and a beautiful evening bathed in spring sunshine.

While Mick warmed up the remains of the chilli, I walked into the town for a recce. 'Don't expect there'll be much going on tonight, but I'll have a quick look,' I told him. As I approached, I could hear the sound of a rock band from one of the bars. It so happened that we had hit Herentals during some sort of musical free-for-all. There was live music in about a dozen different bars and a fiver bought a ticket that gained entry to all of them. There was rock, jazz, blues, funk and all sorts of pop. We sampled most, accompanied with a glass or two of Amstel. In a smoky bar on Nieiuwstraat, a large young man with a moody voice sang blues, accompanying himself on keyboards. In the interval I asked him whether he knew any Van Morrison. Mick had gone to the loo at the time. Halfway through the second half, we were leaning on the bar and tapping our feet when the musician announced, 'Zis one is for ze nice Eenglish boy at the bar' and then broke into a sultry rendition of Haff I Tolt You Ladely That I Luff You. The next morning, we had sore heads. It had been a good night—a very good night, and all the more enjoyable as it was so unexpected. I had thought that Herentals was going to be bolted and shuttered on a Sunday evening. Instead it was alive and throbbing with life and most of its inhabitants singing and dancing on the streets. We were reluctantly leaving Belgium and heading into Holland.

On the way I wanted to make a slight diversion and motor to Turnhout, at the other end of the Dessel-Schoten Kanal, but it was not to be. Our way was blocked by Balen Brug, just a couple of kilometres from the junction, firmly shut on the dot at 4pm. It was Bank Holiday Monday and we'd not passed a commercial all day. We tied to a wooden pontoon and retired to a little café on the opposite bank for a hair of the dog and an apple strudel. The late afternoon was warm and sunny, and we resigned ourselves to a quiet evening. I noticed a gentleman pacing slowly up and down the towpath looking interested in Saul Trader. Then he took out a pad and started to make some notes. People were always admiring the boat, and some had expressed interest in having one built by RWD (that they should seriously consider having a Dutch Barge built in England was somewhat surprising, but a sure testament to the skills of Phil Trotter). 'I think he's making a note of the number of the yard,' I said to Mick, 'maybe he wants to order one.' The details were painted on the side of the wheelhouse.

We drank up and wandered across. Before I had the chance to speak, the gentleman addressed me in a tirade of Flemish. 'Je ne comprends pas,' I protested, but I was getting the message. It didn't take a linguist to understand he was the bridge keeper, this was his bridge, there was his sign stating no mooring for 500m, and he wanted us out—now. His attitude immediately brought out the worst of my pig-headed instincts. He was pissing me off in a big way. We were doing no harm whatsoever, and we wouldn't have been here at all if his bloody bridge hadn't been closed. And we'd be out of his territory and out of his hair first thing in the morning. It's difficult to get your point across when you don't speak a word of Flemish and you're confronted by a stream of abuse from someone who apparently doesn't understand English. It left me with a heavy feeling in the pit of my stomach; all the more a shame after such a fantastic night in Herentals.

He wasn't going to budge. I made an attempt to tie up on the bank opposite, but it was so shallow I couldn't get anywhere near it. Stubbornly I returned to the pontoon. Half an hour later and after another small motor yacht—this one Belgian—had tied up behind me, our gentleman returned. This time it was the Belgian who got the mouthful. Eventually he stormed past screaming 'police police' and making the international hand signal for the telephone with his thumb and little finger. It was getting silly. 'Yes, and my dad's the British ambassador in Brussels,' I shouted after him, pointlessly. Five minutes later a little white Renault 5 van came racing down the towpath, blue light flashing, making that quaint strangled wheezing sound that still ee-ores around the streets of Belgium, like a circus clown on his mono-cycle blowing a trumpet. It was obvious this was one war we were definitely not going to win. The gendarme, looking like the French policeman in the sit-com Allo, was polite and almost apologetic. 'In England you can get stoned half to death by a gang of kids trespassing on a railway bridge and it takes the police half a day to respond,' I told him. 'Here you moor innocently to a pontoon, doing no harm to anyone, and five minutes later you're under arrest.' The Gendarme smiled shyly, probably quietly proud to be complimented on his rapid response. Nevertheless, there was nothing for it but to start up, turn around and (flat out with a trail of blue smoke) make as defiant an exit as was possible in the extremely testing circumstances. 'We don't go far,' said Mick, 'but we do see life!'

We crossed the border almost without realising it and certainly without ceremony. Once again the nasty rumours about the Dutch regulations proved unfounded: 'your radio must conform to blah blah standards' and 'they don't allow hand held radios and will confiscate on sight' and 'you must have a copy of the Deel Almanac (all in Dutch) aboard or you will be arrested'. There were two volumes of the almanac. I never did get the first volume, a weighty tome of rules and regulations, but I did buy a copy of the second as it supposedly contained details of bridge and sluis opening times. Each area was controlled by a different authority, all of which seemed to work to different hours. Obviously, the larger commercial water-ways were open all year round and some even 24 hours a day, but as the size and importance decreased so the hours of working diminished. Frankly I found Deel 2 virtually useless. Apart from being in Dutch (the times and bridge names were decipherable, at least) the information was invariably inaccurate.

At the first Dutch Lock—écluses had now become sluises—the only noticeable difference was the alarm that sounded before the paddles were lifted. I thought a submarine was about to surface. We stopped for the night above the sluis at the virtually unpronounceable 's-Hertogenbosch, a lovely city with a beautiful Gothic Cathedral and the birthplace of Hieronymus Bosch, the 15th century Gothic painter of, to my eye anyway, hideously nightmarish scenes. Some of his characters reminded me of our gentleman bridge keeper of the Brug at Balen. At the large sluis were a number of commercials on the holding pontoon. One by one they slipped into the lock. I motored tentatively forward and as the last commercial passed the gate the light changed to red, and we tied up again. We were about to enter the mighty Maas. The very name conjured up images of gigantic container-laden vessels and huge choppy waves.

Mick went off to the lock keeper's office for a tide table. Once again, as at Merelbeke, the request was met with some amusement and a shrug of the shoulders. 'Ish not important: maybe a few millimetersh and that ish all.' It was over an hour before I saw Mick again, by which time the lock had emptied, filled with another four commercials, and emptied again with Saul Trader as its only passenger. Mick re-joined ship via the lock ladder—the fall was only a few feet—grinning like the cat that'd had the proverbial cream. 'Lovely lady,' he said, waving affectionately in the direction of the cabin. The lovely lady lock keeper had kept him entertained, apparently showing him the intricacies of her job. There were half a dozen CCTV screens on which she could keep a watchful eye on all comings and goings. 'Loved the boat too," he said, still waving and cooing. 'Couldn't believe it wasn't original Dutch. What a lovely lady—shame we haven't got a bit more time.' She had also told him that

Saul Trader 'could go everywhere on the Dutch canals'—a comment which was to prove not quite true.

The images of the Maas were totally accurate. We weren't on it for long. After a few kilometres we had to turn right on to the Heusdens Kanal that connects with the Waal, another mighty water freeway and even busier than the Maas. We crossed the Maas ahead of a huge container carrier, its wheelhouse sitting precariously on top an extended hydraulic ram overlooking the stacked-up load. It looked like an aircraft carrier from where we were and rocked us violently several times as if to say welcome to the real world. We were among the big boys now and we had to behave ourselves and concentrate on not upsetting anybody. Just as we got into position, well to the right on the Waal, we had our first blue board experience. The blue board is exactly that. It is used by large vessels that want to keep in the deep channel by passing on the wrong side—in other words, green to green, starboard to starboard. I wasn't quite clear about all this and asked Tam Murrell for his advice. His emailed reply read, 'As Saul Trader is 21m long, you are classed as a normal vessel within the parameters of the rules of the road.' Comforting to know! What this also meant was that we had to comply with the rules for normal vessels, and this included the blue board rules. The only thing was, at that time I didn't actually have a blue board. The proper ones were about a metre square on a perforated steel plate, light blue with a white border, and stowed horizontal when not in use. Large barges had automatic ones which flipped up at the press of a switch to the vertical position, on the for'ard starboard corner of the wheelhouse roof. They also had a scintillating white light in the centre for use at night or in poor visibility. My rather poor excuse was, in fact, a flag.

The house journal of the Dutch Barge Association was originally called the Blue Flag, presumably because that's what it used to be, and I thought I was sort-of returning to tradition. I had jury-rigged a square of blue plastic sheet and tacked it to a broom handle, with a length of steel pipe sewn into the bottom to keep it vertical. When required, the idea was to slot a broom handle through a couple of brackets on the front of the wheelhouse and 'make a bold alteration to port!' Obviously, it wasn't a great success. The initial problem was that everybody panicked as soon as we had to use it and slotting the handle into the brackets with a trembling hand proved difficult. As we approached a long left-hand bend at Opinen, a 1,000-tonner appeared, ploughing across to our side of the river, blue board sparkling in the sunlight. Christ! What should we do?

Mick dashed outside, and in his haste to unfurl our symbol of professionalism, tripped over the step. By the time he had recovered and fumbled the handle into the sockets, the Dominant had passed us by, nonchalantly and unperturbed. He was actually going into a small harbour and probably didn't even see our token gesture. I thought of Captain Jack Aubrey and the hours his crews would practice firing the great guns aboard his various commands. That's what we needed—practice. But to be honest we didn't get very much at all; everything we passed on our way to Gorinchem seemed quite happy to stay on their own side of the river. We were buffeted and slammed about in the wash as they powered past on their urgent business towards the Rhine. I wasn't sorry when we reached the entrance to the harbour. The weather had turned nasty, with strong wind and rain, and visibility was getting to the scintillating light stage.

As we turned at last into the safety of the outer harbour at Gorinchem, my relief at getting off the busy river was tempered slightly at the apparent lack of an entrance. Then a green light pierced the gloom and a tiny steel gate in the wall started to rise. It looked far too small, but Saul Trader fitted almost perfectly, and we were welcomed by a uniformed harbour master who directed us to a pontoon in the middle of the inner basin. Suddenly we were the big fish in the little pond, the aircraft carrier towering above a tightly packed community of little boats. Gorinchem was Holland, a beautiful little haven surrounded by wonderfully aesthetic rows of buildings, bang in the middle of a small and interesting town of narrow alleys and paved streets, and well worth the 13 Euros per night. We went out on fold-up bikes for a look around and I was accosted by a local copper and warned for cycling the wrong way down a one-way street.

We stayed for a couple of days, and I took the opportunity to have another look at the gauze filter. More gunge needed to be cleaned out, and I was becoming increasingly concerned that there was a problem with the fuel. Maybe we had picked up the dreaded diesel bug. I spoke to Phil. 'It's that shit diesel they sell over there,' was his only offering. I knew it wasn't as simple as that because it had happened first in Devizes, before we had even crossed the Channel. It was more likely to have been the 'shit diesel' in Bradford-on-Avon! Maybe I was just getting paranoid, but it made me reluctant to leave the warmth and security of the harbour for the hostile river. When we ventured out again the weather was almost as hostile—strong winds and rain and choppy water. The channel was marked on each side by beacons, and I was keeping at least 25 to 30ft inside these.

A mile or so from Dordrecht, rolling and pitching in the wash, we struck a submerged object. The boat rose and listed as it ground over with a sickening scrape. It was so bad I immediately rushed below thinking we'd put a hole in the bottom, and somewhat illogically lifted the back cabin floor, half expecting to see a gaping gash with water pouring in. After a heart-stopping few moments, we came to the conclusion that no harm had been done and I made a mental note to report the position to the river authority. I was using the Waterkaarts range of charts for Holland; I had a dozen of them covering most of the country. Although they were large-scale and detailed, I did not find them particularly accurate or clear. Dordrecht was a case in point. There were numerous little havens and entrances, but it was not at all obvious which ones we should use. A large-scale inset plan would have been useful. To add to the mayhem a continuous stream of water buses, operated by modern high-speed super ferries, zoomed backwards and forwards from various other drechts (Pappendrecht, Zwijndrecht. Sliedrecht, Barendrecht and a superfast 45-minute service to Rotterdam). These shark-like beasts skimmed along hardly making any wash at all, and then seconds after they'd passed all hell broke loose. Chairs toppled and we had to hang on for grim death to stay on our feet.

Dordrecht is a very, very busy water junction. It is situated on the left bank of the Oude Maas. To the north the Noord leads to Rotterdam and the Neuw Maas. To the south the Dordste Kil leads into the Hollandsch Diep and the North Sea, while eastwards the route takes the Waal into the Rhine and Germany. The waterborne traffic is continuous day and night. I slowed down to wait for a gap—it was a bit like trying to run across all three lanes of the M1—and then one opened up and we headed into a space. A SeaCat appeared from nowhere, its flashing-orange illuminated destination boards indicating it had come from (or was going to) Pappendrecht. It was on my port quarter and heading for the passenger landing stage. It was overtaking and had me on its give way side. I bit my lip and pressed on, holding my course.

It was my right of way and I hoped he would agree. He slowed and slipped round my stern; probably did the same thing 50 times a day.

The basin we'd entered didn't lead to the canal shown on the chart at all but was a dead end. It was the weekend of the steam extravaganza Dordt in Stoom, and banners everywhere broadcast the fact. I knew there would be many visiting vessels and mooring space at a premium. The biannual event attracted a quarter of a million visitors. Ahead of us a Dutch warship, probably a minesweeper, was tied to a wooden pontoon and there was a space ahead of him. I gently eased Saul Trader alongside. It was a prime spot. I knew it was too good to be true—and it wasn't! Minutes later, before we'd even had a chance to secure the ropes, a powerful launch came roaring over, with the word polizia emblazoned on the side and 'here comes a bollocking' written all over it. Surprisingly the bollocking didn't come. A large policeman was standing with a rope at the stern beneath a large no smoking sign, a cigarette in his mouth, grinning. He offered his rope and asked permission to come alongside. 'Are you coming from Eenglant? From the Norse Zees?' Well, not quite.

The policeman was brilliant. Having explained I wanted to stay for the weekend he first shook his head and said there were 250 boats already in Dordt. He then went ashore and asked the skipper of a vintage tug whether he would mind if we moored alongside him. 'No problems,' he said, 'but please do not scratch the paint.' That would have been difficult as the tug, Happiness, was festooned with a line of thick lorry tyres. The skipper took our lines and proceeded, in the manner of all owners of historic craft and particularly those with historic engines, to tell us all about his beautiful boat.

The festival −attracting hundreds of steam-riven things, not just boats, but traction engines, organs and even full-sized railway engines—was fantastic. One of the highlights was a parade of boats and it was by pure chance that we'd arrived in time. Steamboats of all sizes converged on to the Maas and steamed slowly up and down for about four hours, occasionally breaking into a symphony of whistles. There were tugs, launches, passenger boats, warships, the vintage British passenger steamship Shieldhall and even a couple of Thames slipper launches, all steam-powered and parading around seemingly regardless of each other or of the giant commercials surging through on their urgent passages, that hardly slowed down as they sliced through the melee. Not to be outdone, or to interrupt their exacting schedule, the jet-powered waterbuses zigzagged to and fro, wallowing towards the passenger terminals like frolicking whales. How there were no collisions I really don't know, and it made for a truly remarkable spectacle.

The following day we paid 8 Euros (about £5.50) for a day ticket allowing us to make a circular tour of the entire festival by various forms of vintage transport. The first stage was aboard the SS Success, a superbly restored passenger launch, for a stately cruise downriver to the model arena. We sat back in mahogany and leather vintage opulence, sipping an Americana and letting someone else worry about steering. The model exhibition was housed in a vast warehouse, featuring a display of radio-controlled ships bobbing about on a huge pond surrounded by a road network on which remote-controlled model lorries were loaded by towering remote-controlled model cranes. Someone had recreated the world's largest floating dredger barge: all those thousands of hours of dedicated precision work to end up with something that ugly! In the second hall was a massive OO gauge model railway made up from clubs all over Europe—Britain, Germany, France, Switzerland, Italy, and, of course, Holland and Belgium. Consequently, we could stand at a wayside Italian station and watch TGVs, Swiss Crocodiles, Italian Expresses and the Flying Scotsman all pass through in the space of a few minutes. On a good run, a train would take more than 20 minutes to complete a circuit, assuming it was allowed to do so. Each section was controlled by its respective owner; a bit like the block system of signalling on the real 12in to the foot model. A lady from Hampshire was operating the English section. 'Put on a Bulleid,' I suggested, rather exposing my anorak side. 'I would but we'd probably never get it back,' she replied. 'The last time we sent out the Bournemouth Belle we didn't see it again for more than an hour. It's a bit slow, so the Germans take it off to run their blasted Fleischmann

ICE flat out. It must've been doing a scale 500 miles an hour last time it came through here.'

I wondered what the morning commuters at Micheldever, waiting patiently on the platform for the 6.35am rattler to Waterloo, running 40 minutes late, would make of it as the Berlin-Rome InterCity Express rushed past, scattering the litter and the bowlers. From the exhibition hall, a preserved 4-6-4 tank engine hauled a train to take us to the main railway station, where a fleet of vintage buses plied to and from the docks. On the train I got waylaid by an over- friendly Dutchman; a Calvados–fired friendly Dutchman as it turned out. Roland insisted on sitting with us and telling everyone on the train how much he loved us. 'My father he is prisoner of ze Germans, and YOU have liberated him. Thank you thank you.' To emphasise just how much he appreciated it, he insisted on topping up our coffee with a drop from his flask. He told us all about the happy years he'd spent in Ox Ford Shire and then broke into a rousing chorus of Jerusalem followed by O God Our Help In Ages Past.

Things got worse. To the smug amusement of the other passengers, who sniggered behind their hands, praying he wouldn't notice them and pick on them, Roland produced a camera and insisted on taking a photograph of me, then one of Mick, one of me and Mick together, and then one of all of us. For this he engaged the services of an unsuspecting passer-by looking for a seat. The reluctant camera operator was Heinrich, unfortunately a German.

Heinrich temporarily deflected the heat. 'Zees people are Eenglish—they liberated my country from you, and I love zed. Please will you promise me that you will not inwade my country again.'

Heinrich looked perplexed. He was cursing his luck at having walked into this one and, to be honest, I don't think he had any intention of invading Holland. Roland then went into a thunderous version of Deutchland Uber Alles—all eight verses! Gott im Himmel! We suddenly found an absorbing fascination with the suburbia passing the window. I was thinking we were going to be lumbered with Roland and was working out a way of giving him the slip, but I needn't have worried. The guard came into the carriage with the call for tickets and suddenly, Roland was gone. Considering his size and his payload of Calvados, he moved like lightning. I contemplated reporting him to the guard but thought better of it. We'd had enough fun for one day.

As we left the train, I caught sight of Roland spread-eagled on a wooden bench on the platform, dead to the world, his Calvados clutched to his chest and snoring loudly. 'Roland Rat,' said Mick, 'for Christ's sake, don't wake him up. We don't go far but we do see life!'

There was a queue of vintage buses in the station concourse. Patriotically we jumped aboard a Leyland Royal Tiger and was returned sedately to dock. We spent the rest of the weekend wandering among the bars and stalls. Around every corner was a stage with a band of some sort and folk groups adding to the atmosphere. There were model traction engines, proud owners sitting astride their charges and enjoying the fruits of their thousands of hours' worth of patient and dedicated labour. Open trailers full of laughing children were towed behind. Full-sized traction engines, hot with the smell of oil and steam, simmered on the docksides, and there were displays of all kinds of ancient tools and engines, and a trailer with about 50 vintage Seagull outboard motors hanging from rails. In the Wolvershaven, packed with an atmospheric collection of historic craft sympathetically floodlit for effect, we were treated to a wonderful symphony of hooting and whooping from the assembled whistles. In one corner was moored a whole fleet of Botters, small traditional fishing craft with tanned sails, some of which had been converted as camping skiffs. On the Sunday evening, after most of the exhibits had steamed away, we moved Saul Trader in to the Wolvershaven itself. It nestled shyly alongside, feeling a bit of an imposter among such illustrious company but was nevertheless graciously accepted by these venerable craft. Amazingly, Dordtrecht is twinned with my hometown of Hastings, although what they had in common, I couldn't begin to imagine.

My brother came over for the next stage with Knocker and Shirley, some friends from Salisbury. Roy, ever the perfectionist, wasn't happy with the fuel filtering system. Neither was I, for that matter. The idea of slopping around out of control out on the mighty river was not conducive to peace of mind. The last thing I wanted was the engine to give up the ghost in mid-stream with a heaving convoy of commercials bearing down on all sides—the stuff of nightmares. Roy decided the answer was to put another filter in the line between the tank and the hand-prime pump. Once this small extra safeguard was in place, we set off on the Maas for Rotterdam with renewed confidence. It was June but it felt more like February. Shirley braved a deckchair on the foredeck for an hour or so but eventually succumbed. Rotterdam arrived somewhat sooner than expected, and again the chart was found a bit wanting on the choice of mooring places.

There were several harbours, but they all seemed a bit unwelcoming. I nosed the boat into the entrance of the Leuvehaven near the Maritime Museum, but it looked extremely tight for space, so we backed out and tied to the wall, bouncing in the wash, while I went to ask for advice. We passed beneath the impressive and futuristic Erasmus Brug and had a look at the small Veerhaven. This would have been ideal but unfortunately there was a boat rally taking place and all the spaces had been taken. We finally arrived at the Parkhaven at the entrance to the Delftse Schie Canal. It was some way from the centre and directly under the shadow of the Euro Mast. We walked back to explore the Maritime Museum and after a shower donned our glad rags (a rare experience) and ate in the New Ocean Paradise Floating Chinese Restaurant, a very large and impressive establishment with a view high above the river. As we divided the numerous dishes between us, we watched a 500-ton liquid gas carrier pass beneath and squeeze itself between Saul Trader and into the lock with inches to spare. In the morning Roy and I went skywards in the Euro Tower. The top half was a capsule which took off like a space rocket and slowly revolved its way to the top around a central spindle, thus affording panoramic views of the city. Saul Trader looked like a Matchbox toy.

We sailed at noon bound for Leiden. We were on the cut again and it was relatively calm. To enter Leiden harbour, we turned left on to the Ould Rhin at a crossroads, passing lines of moored craft of all descriptions and, after waiting for a remotely controlled bridge to open, we were directed to a mooring. Leiden, a town of some 12,0000 souls, was intersected by a myriad of small canals. Leiden University is the oldest in the Netherlands and it is fittingly twinned with Oxford, the oldest university in England. The two branches of the Old Rhine, which entered Leiden on the east, united in the centre of the town, which sat at the confluence of the Old and New Rhines and hosted numerous festivals and events throughout the year. In October it celebrates the Relief of Leiden after the siege of the city during the Eighty Days War in 1574, when costumed pageants and marching bands precede the dishing out of herring and white bread. In May there was a barrel organ festival, which we'd just missed. More importantly, to us anyway, there was another festival about to happen. The World Cup had started, and we were hoping against hope there just may be a bar sympathetic to our cause. Holland had not qualified, and we wondered whether the Dutch might have been turned off to the idea. The following day Ireland were playing Germany at 8am, and it was highly unlikely that anyone in Leiden would be remotely interested. The best way to explore this sort of situation was in the dinghy, so off we went on a waterborne safari around the tree-lined (and bar-lined) avenues of Leiden.

There is such a spider's web network of inner canals that we got completely lost. After an hour spent literally going around in circles, we were on the point of having to embarrassingly ask the way back. Then we turned a corner and there in front of us, like an oasis in the desert, shone a neon light announcing the Crazy Horse Irish pub. Over a pint of Murphy's—well, you can't have everything—the Dutch barman told us Leiden had a thriving Irish population and would be opening at 7am to serve an Irish fry-up for the match. Result or what! Ireland drew with the mighty Germans, getting the equaliser in the very last minute in dramatic circumstances. The Irish (and the Dutch) went berserk, and the barman immediately played Danny Boy at full blast over the stereo system. It was the most emotional moment I've ever had at 8.30am! England were playing the Argentines the following afternoon. They won 1-0, a memorable victory with Beckham scoring from the spot, and this time the barman lined up We Are The Champions for the 200-decibel treatment. We had got to like Leiden.

As we left the following morning, the bridge keeper shouted something I didn't catch. With the irritating habit of someone who has never handled a floating object of any kind, he did so at a time which made it impossible to slow down enough to hear him without losing all steerage and ending up broadside across the Cut. I nodded, dismissing the information as something I probably didn't need to hear anyway... an almost fatal mistake. At the crossroad, we turned left to head north. Immediately after the turn there was another lift bridge, the Spanjaardsbrug, which was in the horizontal position and the red light on. After a few minutes, the road barriers came down and hordes of mopeds and motor scooters on their urgent way to work lined up against the barrier like riders at the start of a speedway race. Up came the bridge but the light stayed on red.

We waited. And waited. Still red. There was definitely nothing coming from the opposite direction. The bridge must have been raised for us. I put Saul Trader into gear, and we moved slowly forwards, gathering speed. Then, when we were about 20m or so from the bridge and past the point of no return, Roy shouted in panic. 'It's coming down!' I had seen it too, but it was too late to stop. I opened the throttle and prayed that the filter wouldn't choose this moment to block. It was a frightening few seconds, during which time all sorts of scenarios flashed through my mind. Was this what the bridge keeper had been trying to tell me? The clearance with the bridge in the lowered position was about 3ft. God knows what would have happened had we been trapped. Would we have sunk? I had a momentary flashback of the wheelhouse splintering at Tewkesbury. The moped jockeys bent forward on their handlebars, wide eyes staring from under their helmets and revving their engines, as we literally shot through the rapidly reducing aperture and into safety. I felt the blood drain from my face, and I had to sit down. I was shaking uncontrollably.

What had happened? The bridge was unmanned but we were obviously under the surveillance of CCTV. Was there a fault? Why was the bridge raised in the first place? Did the bridge keeper assume I was going to get through and started to lower to save a bit of time? We would never know. It reinforced my theory though: never take anything for granted. When I thought about it logically, I realised the bridge keeper was trying to tell me that the light was kaput, but one thing was for sure—I wouldn't be passing red lights again. It had left me feeling quite ill.

Chapter 10

Amsterdam

A T BUITENKAARD we turned right on to the Ring-vaart d.v.Haarlemermeerpolder Canal. Why the hell couldn't they have names like us? What's wrong with Oxford or Trent and Mersey? We filled the water tanks for 50 Eurocents per 100 litres. I remembered cursing the first time we'd been forced to actually pay for water in England. There was an old joke that went, 'water—it'll never sell.' Little did they know!

I had changed my plans again. The barman at the Crazy Horse had said, 'Ijmuiden—why would anyone want to go to Ijmuiden?' I took him at his word, and we headed instead straight for Amsterdam. Mrs Bradshaw reported, 'Oosterdok—good—close to station, museum and centre.' I found the Oosterdok on the chart after much searching with my printer's magnifying glass. It was on the north side and looked as though we could get there via the canal system through the centre of the city. We passed through a small inland lake, the Nieuwe Meer, and into the sluis. This was the entrance to the Amsterdam Canals and here we had to wait for several commercials. The lock keeper checked the papiers and I paid 12 Euros for a three-day stay in the city. It was 5pm. 'You will wait outside the next bridge until 6pm,' he told me. 'We are closing all the bridges for the peak hours.'

That seemed fair enough. We passed the stadium that had hosted the 1928 Olympic Games and tied on the wall opposite a fascinating tram depot. It was built inside a triangular junction of two waterways and consisted of a massive shed with at least 30 'roads' fed by a huge turning circle in the shape of a dew drop. It reminded me of the large engine sheds of old, except that instead of Kings and Castles shunting back and forth, these were super trams, articulated and plastered with advertising liveries, gliding past with practised precision to slide into their allotted space in the shed to await their next turn of duty. Watching them clattering in and out, I felt a sadness that we had demolished our eco-friendly public transport systems 40 years before and had only just woken up to the fact it was a big mistake. Most major continental cities had a modernised trolleybus or tram network that was clean, efficient and affordable. Every day these trams run to exactly the same timetable; they could do it with their eyes closed.

We did a bit of shopping while we waited. On our return at 5.55pm three commercials had appeared and had already cast off, impatiently revving their engines inches from the bridge. We followed suit and joined the back of the line. On the dot of six, the bridge raised, engines roared in clouds of smoke, and we were off. It was like the start of the Monaco Grand Prix—flat out through narrow streets lined with four and five-storey buildings each with individual gable ends. The canal was only about the width of two commercials, but they surged ahead, and I had to keep the throttle at 1,500 revs to keep up. And I had to keep up as there were about ten bridges, one after the other, raising in sequence to keep the convoy moving and avoid holding up the traffic for no minute longer than necessary. It was like passing through a guard of honour at a wedding. A luxury motor yacht appeared right behind us. He was obviously faster but there was no way I was going to let him pass as that would put me last in the queue and I was dreading the sight of a bridge coming down in front of me.

At one point everything slowed—no brake lights here—and we all converged, veering sideways in an attempt to stop in a straight line. Two big ones were coming the other way and there was only just enough room to pass. It was quite exhilarating but there wasn't much chance of admiring the view. It was difficult enough to keep track of exactly where we were; I was looking for a junction where I thought we could cut through to the

Oosterdok by the back door. We found what looked like an entrance and turned in. There was a quaint lift bridge that looked as though it hadn't been moved in years. We waited for more than 20 minutes before concluding it probably wouldn't be moving for another 20 years. Once again, the chart was incorrect, or certainly not very clear.

We reluctantly backed out and continued through another two or three bridges into the vast expanse of the Markermeer. This was ocean liner territory, and there were vessels crisscrossing from all directions. We passed beneath the shadow of the 50,000-ton Crystal Symphony and gratefully dived below the railway station and into the Oosterdok. To the left there was a small marina with lines of pontoons. I made for an empty space. Before we made it alongside, a head appeared from a hatch to tell us it was a private mooring.

'Where do we go?' I asked and was answered with a shrug before the head disappeared below again. To the right of the entrance was a modernistic curving foot-bridge. It was touch and go as to whether we could get under it. At one end was a lift bridge in the horizontal position. I optimistically called up the Oosterdok control on the radio and was surprised when they answered. 'Could you lift the bridge for me please?' 'For sure—one moment please.' Wow. The bridge slowly raised but the light stayed on red. We waited; I wasn't going to be caught out like that again. And waited. And waited. The bridge stayed up and the light stayed red. I got back on the radio. 'What shall I do?' I pleaded. 'The bridge is ready, but the light is red.' 'Oh this is OK—don't worry about him—the light he has not been vorking for tree weeks now!' Sometimes you just can't bloody win.

Amsterdam lived up to its name—city of the free—where you could smoke pot and make love at will! The city of a thousand streets and a thousand canal bridges that all look exactly the same. I remembered coming here in the late 1960s trying to impress a girlfriend. It wasn't very successful. On the first night we left our hotel for an early evening stroll and got hopelessly lost. I hadn't made a note of the name of the hotel and it took us about four hours to find it, by which time we were too knackered to go out again. There was a story about someone in a similar situation who took the precaution of writing down the name of the street from a sign on the corner where his hotel was located. After a good night out, he got into a cab, pulled the crumpled piece of paper from his pocket and confidently announced, 'eingang strasse danke please!' It translated to one-way street.

We window-shopped in the sleazy red velvet-curtained backstreets, where merchandise came in all shapes, sizes and hues. We did a waterbus tour into the interior canals forbidden to Saul Trader and drank too much in smoky nightclubs. We drew a line at smoking pot, however, on the grounds that it probably wasn't conducive to navigating amongst cruise liners. And we got mugged! At least I got mugged. At some ungodly hour of the morning my brother and I were accosted by a couple of eastern European gentlemen offering their little sisters, and during the animated discussion—throughout which, I hasten to add, we were adamantly refusing all offers—my credit cards were liberated from the pocket of my body warmer in a flash, never to be seen again. And that, basically, was how Amsterdam was for me. I spent the following day trying to get cash with the only credit card I still had, American Express, and the money changers didn't want to know. Nor did the banks. I finally found an American Express office and managed to get myself back in funds. My brother caught the train, dead on time at 9.05am, to Antwerp and Oostende, and we motored out of the Oosterdok with few regrets, leaving the great metropolis to the tourists and the muggers. I found Amsterdam a bit threatening. I suppose the mugging didn't help but there seemed too many dubious-looking people hanging around for my liking.

We followed the buoys and the procession of commercials on to the Amsterdam-Rijnkanaal to Rijswijk, where we forked left on to the Nederrijn towards Arnhem and where I intended to leave the boat for a few weeks. Knocker took the wheel and I knocked up a very nice stir fry from the last of the food. The river flowed swiftly through the centre and all the moorings were taken up by the massive Rhine cruisers. We pushed across the flow into a sheltered harbour, shown on the chart as the Nieuwhaven. I tried calling the harbour master for advice, but it was a Saturday and I got no reply. We found a space alongside a bank with a couple of bollards and tied behind three residential vessels rafted together. The next priority was to find a friendly bar; England was playing Denmark in the next phase of the World Cup. The centre of Arnhem was about two miles away and was heaving with Saturday shoppers. The myriad of narrow streets, lined with individual, classy, and probably very expensive shops, were thronging. There was only one thing missing: any form of bar, and we were starting to panic. Kick-off was half an hour away. 'I think this place might be run by Quakers,' I said to Knocker. 'What do you mean—a good place to get your oats?'

I approached a young man selling the Dutch equivalent of The Big Issue, who told us of a street which was nothing except bars and to there we beelined. There was the ubiquitous Irish bar but not a screen in sight. This was getting desperate. Opposite we entered an unlikely glitzy-looking chrome and neon sort of place. It was completely deserted apart from Jules the barman. In the middle of the floor stood a huge TV set balanced on a makeshift stand, draped with the cross of St. George. 'Football's coming home,' said Knock, 'there is a God.' 'This does look like our sort of bar,' I agreed. 'Ah yes, I am Jules. I am Dutch and a very, very big England fan.' A little corner in some foreign field. We settled back. Jules brought the drinks and England were 3-nil up at half-time, each goal accompanied by the obligatory refrain of We Are The Champions. This was living alright! After the game I caught the train to Dordrecht to pick up the car, and early the next morning we were on our way to Dunkirk, and dear old Norfolk Line.

The following week I was driving in the middle of Gloucestershire when my mobile rang. 'Thiss iss the Harbour Masster Arnhem here—my name iss Jan.' Uh-oh. 'Your vessel it is Shaul Trader? It musst be mauved. It is an obstruction in the harbour.' Apparently, it was in an area where commercials loading grain needed to move backwards and forwards under the elevator and there was a grain shipment imminent. I apologised profusely and explained my position. 'Well we will haff to mauve your boat with a tug,' said Jan, 'but this will be very expensive. I will see what we can do and telephone tomorrow.'

The following day, Jan rang as promised. 'Well there are two things which we can do,' he said. 'First we can mauve the vessel with the tug. Cost five hundred Euros.' Christ! 'Or the other thing is I have a friend who has his own vessel and he will mauve it for you—cost—nothing!' He emphasised the word nothing. A comedian as well as a harbour master with a feel for the melodramatic. I toyed with the idea of asking for time to think about it, but I thought the joke might be lost in translation and didn't want to jeopardise the offer. 'Well I think we'll go for the second option then,' I said, after a pause, 'but I must find some way to thank your friend.' 'Of course,' Jan replied. 'I think some whisky will be very good.' Job done—and to the total satisfaction of all concerned.

I returned a couple of weeks later armed with two bottles of 12-year-old Glenfiddich, the best Norfolk Line duty-free could provide. Jan was gracious in his acceptance and no harm had been done to Anglo–Dutch relations.

Chapter 11

Friesland

WHEN WE returned—Roy, Scragg and I—Saul Trader had been 'mauved' to the outside of the three residential boats, and the 1,000 tons of grain had been successfully loaded and dispatched. We went to find Jules, but the bar was boarded and shuttered. Sadly, it had not paid its way and closed down—not really surprising on the strength of the crowd for the England game, but sad all the same. We had to make do with the Irish bar where we were mobbed by a very large Arnhem supporter who insisted on plying us with drink and regaling us with stories of his sojourns to English football grounds.

'Ah yess—Port Man Road—Arnold Muhren—Eepswich Town ya—Paul Mariner—great shide ya,' he said. When I confessed to having more than a passing interest in Southampton, he was no slouch either. 'Shaint Maries Frenss Prowident Schtadium, Masshew Le Tishier—great player, Micky Channon—great player.' He pronounced each word with the stucco precision of a passionately inebriated Dutch follower of English football, eager to show off his considerable knowledge. My feeble attempt at a rally of trivia about the Dutch game—Johann Cruyff... Patrick Kluivert... Total Football—broke down rather pathetically in midfield.

The next day we had another close encounter of the blue board kind. I could still not really understand why it was the upstream vessel that normally instigated the pass-on-the-left signal. After all it was the downstream boat that had the right of way. We were heading downstream on the Ijssell, and on the first right-hand bend we were confronted by a large commercial, plumb in the middle of the river and its blue board flashing merrily. Roy dashed out with our makeshift flag and stuck it up, while I wound the wheel to port and crossed his bow. As we passed, with 20ft or so to spare, the sun disappeared, and everything went dark. I glanced over my left shoulder and there, towering above us, were the massive bows of another commercial, which was overtaking us. The result was a Saul Trader sandwich—with 2,000 tons of bread and no room for any relish! The overtaking boat crashed by, the wife with a hand lightly caressing her joystick (if you'll pardon the expression), waving with mild amusement at our rather pathetic gesture. I resolved there and then that we *must* do something about our ridiculous flag.

We spent the night against the wall at Zutphen below the constantly thundering railway bridge. All night long we felt the surge of passing commercials speeding up and down the river, arrogantly sweeping under the bridge with inches to spare. At the far side was a lifting span but ironically it was the yachts with their masts stepped that were the only vessels requiring an interruption to the railway timetable. At Spoolde we turned off the river again into the Zwaartwater, the inland system that would eventually take us into Friesland. At Zwolle the harbour was full of motorboats and yachts. The harbour master insisted there was room for us at the far end in the centre of the town, so I turned Saul Trader around and slowly reversed past millions of pounds worth of moulded plastic with the harbour master waving encouragement like a parking attendant eager to capitalise on every inch of space. Opposite us was a sleek and shiny motor yacht which Scragg confidently informed us was a Feretti. Price? If you need to ask, you won't be able to afford! Scragg could accurately identify any model of yacht at a mile and a half. 'That's a Broom 45, here comes a Duster 24—they are wank!' He had an interesting turn of phrase, did Scragg. It did look somewhat incongruous in the middle of Zwolle, this Feretti, and would have been more at home moored stern on to the quay at Monte Carlo, but strange as it seemed, having come so far inland, we were only a few kilometres from the Ijssellmeer, the huge inland sea which led to Amsterdam and the North Sea itself.

Holland is so full of water; inland seas, vast navigable lakes and deep-water canals allowing very large sea-going vessels to penetrate far inland and traverse the country from one side to the other. Occasionally a passing barge carried the slogan 'Keeping 40 lorries off the roads.' A sobering thought, and that was just the smaller ones. I had counted a hundred 40ft containers on some of the Rhine-bound vessels passing Dordrecht—that's one hundred lorries in anyone's language.

In Meppel we came across a novel form of pub entertainment: the music was provided by computer. The landlord, Arnolt, proudly explained he was connected to an online music site which gave instant access to some 50,000 songs. The game was to put it to the test, each bar-propper selecting some obscure dusty rock classic and then joining in raucously as it was belted out through the bar's audio system. I went for a relatively easy one, Bob Dylan's Forever Young. We sang our hearts out and at one stage, one of the local wags distributed an orange into which he stuck a plastic knife to simulate a microphone which we waved about in the fashion of Tom Jones as we performed our favourite numbers. It was good fun—the sort of good fun that results in swaying back to the boat in the small hours and a headache for breakfast.

After Meppel the canal became narrower and quieter and we suddenly realised we hadn't seen a commercial all day. The bridges were manned but I was still wary about passing through, especially on the ones where the bridgeman was out of sight. Once again, this restricted progress, as they closed down for the night at 5pm. This meant we had to make a forced stop at Dieverbrug, where the only diversion was the most expensive Chinese restaurant in the world. It was very nice and obviously very popular, but at 140 Euros for the three of us—crab soup, prawns in oyster sauce and a couple of beers each—I didn't put it on the list of must-do-agains.

At Assen we tried to get into the town. Mrs Bradshaw was somewhat vague, saying merely, 'Centre'. We passed through the deep Peelosluis. Will, the lock keeper, told us that the entrance to the town arm was half a mile further on. After waiting at the first bridge for something to happen, some local walkers pointed out a button on the side of the pontoon. This had the desired effect and accompanied by bells and whistles, we proceeded. At the next bridge one would naturally assume the same procedure. We searched high and low but there was no magic button. There was a telephone number and I rang this to be told by the controller that we didn't really want to go into the town as the walls were very high and mooring was difficult but instead he would make an exception for us and inform the lock keeper at Peelosluis to let us moor there. The only problem with that was that it was about two miles from the town.

Roy was leaving to go back to work and Mick was going to join us. The logistical problems were soon solved by a friendly and efficient taxi service. For lock keeper Will, this was a summer job. The Dutch canals we were now sailing were purely for leisure use, only open during the summer season. Each area had its own rules as far as opening times and this was not clearly indicated on the chart or in the Deel Almanac, a fact that was to cause a few problems towards the end of the summer. We caught the train to Arnhem and Roy was duly exchanged at Dunkirk for Mick.

It was early August and for the first time it was warm enough to get the legs out. We sat outside an upmarket café in Assen listening to modern jazz. Summer had finally arrived. We transited Peelosluis for the third time and said our farewells to Will with a bottle of wine, which he accepted with some embarrassment. We were now heading for Friesland, home of black and white cows, horses and windmills, and where they indulge in some rather strange pastimes. In winter they race around frozen canals on skates on the Elfstedentocht 200km circuit that passes eleven cities! In summer they go wadlopening; wading across the WaddenZee. And then there's fierl-jeppening, the strangest of them all, where they run at a pole, jump at it and try to get to the top before it topples over and dumps them into a pile of sand. It takes all sorts.

The first stop was at Groningen. 'You haff arrived at a very exciting time,' the young summer bridge keeper delighted in telling us. He'd taken the trouble of cycling down to the boat after we had found a mooring right in the heart of this beautiful Bohemian town. Wadloping, I wondered, or fierljeppening? 'It is the annual festival and tonight is the first night of our celebrations,' he explained. I asked him what sort of entertainment was on offer. 'Oh, it is everything. We haff music of all dimensions, dancing and tea-etter and also we haff the most very funny comedians of all Hollansch.' Judging by the thousands who thronged the park, standing in front of the hundreds of small booths and bursting their sides, they must have been hilarious. Unfortunately watching a comedian who is speaking in Dutch can be a bit frustrating when you don't speak any.

Fortunately there were lots of other dimensions, and we enjoyed some jazz and a pop band playing on the side of an illuminated lake, masses of small craft exhibitions and a huge obscene waffle topped with honey and cream which oozed everywhere like molten lava, and the buzz of people enjoying the balmy atmosphere. We joined the tail of a queue to see the Comedy Circus, though why did they advertise it in English and lull you into a false sense of security? It was obvious the whole show was going to be in Dutch. 'It's Groningen under the weight of all these people,' said Scragg, dead pan. That was the funniest thing we heard all night! We sat on the grass with a schooner of Warsteiner, under the stars and the fairy lights, and hummed to the strains of a Beach Boys soundalike band. They were trusting and old-fashioned enough in Holland to let people sit outside with real glasses—none of your Tupperware beer cups here, unlike England where you're forced to drink from irritatingly thin containers. The celebrations were set to go on for another week. We could never have survived with all that excitement, so we set off in search of another fairyland.

Scragg made himself useful and made a new blue board for us, in the proper shade of blue and carrying a white border. A length of half-inch copper pipe was attached to the back, which slid into a couple of plastic pipe holders screwed into the wheelhouse. Job done! We had to twist it up and down manually and we didn't have an oscillating light, but it was a great improvement on the plastic flag. Many years later we had to have the boat surveyed and inspected for the newly implemented European Boat Safety Certificate, or TRIWV as it was known. This inspection was carried out by a Dutch ship surveyor who stipulated a number of jobs to be done in order to comply. Strangely, never once did he mention the blue board!

Summer had arrived with a vengeance and the steel decks were too hot to walk on in bare feet. We followed a replica Tjalk through a railway swing bridge and headed northwards towards the Riet deep. No commercial traffic now, although we were reminded at the junction with the Dtarkenborgh Kanaal that inland shipping is never far away in Holland. After the lock, our course crossed the main line, a sort-of Groningen bypass, and part of a route connecting Harlingen on the Waddenzee with Delfzijl on the eastern tip of Friesland. Here a 1,000-tonner appeared from nowhere, causing the Tjalk, which had left the lock ahead of us, to slam on the brakes to avoid a collision.

We passed several boats anchored in the beautiful Lauwersmeer and decided we should do the same. As we approached a small wooden landing stage, the incumbent very considerately decided to leave, and we jumped into bed while it was still warm. The water wasn't quite so warm but lovely once you were in. We swam for an hour and Scragg washed his hair, there being an X in the month, and we sunbathed on the deck and enjoyed a prawn salad, fresh that morning from the market in Groningen. That's what barging's all about.

That evening we tied up in the small town of Dokkum and the following day, we made an enforced stop at Birdaard while the bridge keeper had his lunch. The setting was pure Holland and I realised these enforced stops could be quite advantageous. We strolled around the pretty, quiet village in the sunshine, sat in a bar beside the bridge for omelettes and beer, and toured the ancient De Zwaluw corn mill with Hildegaard, our energetic guide. We followed her breathlessly up and down precarious ladders to view machinery while she explained the history and the workings of the mill in perfect English. It was struck by lightning and burnt down in 1972, and restoration was completed in 1988. Although originally intended as a static exhibit, the mill was by now fully operational and ground corn on a daily basis. Surprisingly, Scragg, who climbed the tower crane at Saul like a cat, was very dubious about walking around the platform deck of the windmill. Hildegaard was a somewhat robust lady. 'It can't be safe,' he wimped, 'it'll never take her weight, will it?'

In Leuwarden we toured around before finding the only available mooring space, for which we were charged eight Euros. There was something about the place I didn't like, probably not helped by the weather which had become grey and overcast, and this feeling was accentuated somewhat after our customary dinghy tour. Although nothing untoward happened and my fears were probably totally unfounded, the town gave me an uneasy feeling. We passed through a labyrinth of dark dank tunnels, some of which were so low that we had to duck our heads. Upon emerging from one of them into the gloom, we found ourselves in a seedy looking area where haggard and unhealthy-looking females in tatty miniskirts leant against doorways, their faces made pallid by the glare of light bulbs painted red above their heads. Even more seedy and dangerous looking men lurked menacingly, watching over their charges. This was not the place to linger. It was all a bit sad and neglected. That night we locked the doors and ate aboard. Maybe I misjudged the place; in fact, I read another barging book by Joe May, who absolutely adored the town. I must say that we didn't really have a good look around.

The night passed peacefully without incident, and the next morning we headed west for the Waddenzee port of Harlingen. We followed the Van Harinx Kanaal to Harlingen, and the trip was mostly uneventful. The lift bridges on this stretch used the traditional method of collecting the toll. The keeper would hang out of his cabin with a fishing rod with a clog swinging on the end and dangle it in front of you for payment. At first, we were confused as to how much we had to pay. Was it an arbitrary donation? At the first bridge we dropped in two Euros and, as no alarm bells rang, we assumed it had been accepted by the beaming 'bruggie'. At the next we realised why he had looked so pleased with himself. We noticed a sign some 100m from the bridge clearly stating: 'Brug passage one Euro.' It was just as well that we noticed this when we did. It saved us a small fortune as there were quite a few more bridges ahead. At one, the keeper leant out of his window on our approach and started frantically waving his arms about, keeping up a ceaseless vitriol in flowing Dutch. I slowed and tried to decipher what it was he was so urgently trying to tell us. There was certainly nothing coming the other way, I wasn't making a wash, I hadn't inadvertently got my navigation lights on, there was no signs of a fire and my flies weren't undone! I gave up and still he ranted. As we passed, I called up in my best BBC English, 'Do you speak English because I certainly don't speak Dutch.' We never discovered what was troubling him.

At Harlingen, an important port on the Waddenzee, we couldn't get anywhere near the harbour for sailing Tjalks, most of which are used for chartering. Ferries operate from here to Amsterdam. We watched the Tjalks expertly sail in and out between the piers, window-shopped in the town and found a bar with Murphy's on tap. In the evening we explored in the dinghy and worked out the exit route. We could have turned around and gone back to Leeuwarden, but that seemed a bit negative. We could have ventured on to the Waddenzee and passed through the hole in the Afsluitdjik via the Lorentzsluisen, but that seemed a bit too adventurous. The alternative was the much smaller gauge Harlingervaart, which led south east to Bolsward, and that's the one we chose.

The bridge leading out of Harlingen stayed firmly closed. We talked with an elderly couple on a retired commercial who told us it would be open at 1pm. We also gathered from them that it might be touch and go for us to get through the Harlingervaart but the guide indicated that with the wheelhouse lowered, we should be OK. At 1pm on the dot the bridge raised, and we had to turn tight left. The bridge keeper looked nonplussed and gave no hint as to his feelings one way or another about these mad English venturing into the unknown. Immediately as we straightened ourselves after the bridge there was another, 7ft or so above the waterline and definitely not to be moved. So down came the wheelhouse for the first time since the Kennet & Avon. It was very shallow, and we made slow progress. Some fishermen looked at us with mild surprise, but we crept on. At Arum there was a crossroad. After a quick glance at the chart I decided to go straight on, but we soon realised that was a mistake and had to reverse 400m after going aground. By the time we got to the village of Witmarsum, we were really ditch crawling. It looked more and more daunting.

A sharp right-hander under a low concrete bridge set at an obtuse angle, past a row of neat houses and then another sharp left-hand bend under another bridge. There were a couple of cabin cruisers tied on the starboard side just before the bridge, which just left enough room to squeeze by. It felt like the North Stratford canal. We were on tick-over; the bottom felt very close. I got the bow under the bridge, with about three inches of headroom. I was about to crouch down to avoid hitting my head when we stopped. The bow was tight into the left-hand bank. The stern was just about touching the starboard side, and we were well and truly jammed. I tried backwards—no go. I tried forwards—same thing. I tried backward with revs and then forward immediately—nothing. It was teatime; I could see the flicker of the TV sets inside the little houses, but a crowd gathered. People started to come out to see what the fuss was about. Some brought their tea with them, and some returned quickly for their cameras. Some even had video cameras! This was going to be quite a show. Not a lot happened in Witmarsum—that was obvious.

Scragg tied our two longest ropes together and clambered ashore. All fit and able villagers grabbed the line as it stretched ahead and heaved together. I motored gently, and they grunted and strained. After several attempts it was plain this was achieving nothing. Without having to be asked, a friendly neighbour appeared triumphantly in a Suzuki four-wheeler. In retrospect I should have realised that a tug of war between a one-ton Jeep and a 60-ton barge wasn't going to be fair sides. At one point, as the rope stretched to breaking point, I thought the Jeep was going to come flying backwards as if on a length of elastic and dive straight into the cut!

It was starting to get dark, so I thanked him for trying and more or less resigned myself to staying where we were for the night. At that point another gentleman stepped out of the crowd. 'I am ze farmer here and I haff a big tractor—would you like me to fetch this?' We were ready to try anything. I still had reservations but there weren't a vast number of alternatives. When it arrived, the tractor turned out to be one of those huge things with wheels like a Tonka Toy—the sort of thing they bring out during rush hour in England towing a giant baler just to annoy the locals. What's more, attached to the rear was a hydraulic arm. It was Scragg who, remembering the episode at Limpley Stoke, realised what we needed to do. Instead of attaching the rope to the back of the tractor, he connected it to the arm and used the hydraulics to slowly swivel it gently round. Saul Trader literally inched forward to great cheers and arm-waving from the crowd of locals which, by now, included the entire village. After a couple of adjustments to the angle, and a few more moments of breath-holding, we squeezed through the bridge and out into a short straight section of the canal. The crowd went wild. Cameras flashed, videos whirred, and everybody clapped and shouted. It was like a carnival.

The farmer was the secretary of the local Save Our Canal lobby group and was delighted we'd made the effort to get through. 'This will be reported to the newspaper,' he told me excitedly. 'It will be another string in our bow to get this canal properly dredged.' Oh good, we'd helped somebody out then. I gave him a bottle of wine in thanks. 'You'll have to share it,' I told him.

Phew! We hadn't had as much fun since England. What was next? As we motored slowly into the gloom, I noticed a couple of dozen cyclists silhouetted in the light of the glowing sunset, riding in line across the flat landscape. 'Perfect Dutch scene,' I said to Scragg, 'families out for a quiet evening cycle ride.' When we reached the next bridge, some 2km away, I realised where they had been heading—there they all were, lined up on the bridge, waiting for another disaster. How they cheered as we passed through without incident, bless their little Dutch cotton socks! I'm sure they'd come to help us again if necessary—not to gloat and snigger at our plight. Nice people, bloody nice people.

But we then made another fatal mistake, having been lulled into a false sense of security and believing we'd got over the worst. Half an hour later, we lost steerage again and ran onto the mud. While trying to reverse out, the rudder dislodged and bent the steel bar that connects it to the hydraulic ram. The damage was so bad it was impossible to steer. We were close to giving up at that stage. But Scragg, not to be beaten, managed to straighten it enough to enable us to limp into Bolsward, too late for the town bridge and anyway, too knackered to want to do any exploring.

A new day and new hope. By pure chance we had moored outside a small industrial estate. Scragg took the bent bar to a jobbing foundry, and the owner very kindly put it into his press and flattened it perfectly. And he wouldn't take a cent for it; we had to insist that he accepted something for his trouble. Bloody nice people. 'Ee was alright,' Scragg conceded, 'but why do these people have to talk so wank—why can't they speak proper?'

We got water and stores in Bolsward, and the following night was spent in Workum, a popular little town on the Ijsselmeer—so popular that finding a mooring space among the hundreds of steel cruisers was almost impossible. We took the dinghy to have a look at the entrance into the Ijsselmeer and, having looked at the chart, decided we would put to sea. The next morning, we motored out of the harbour and into the Ijsselmeer. The weather was fine, but a fresh westerly breeze was blowing which chopped up the waves to three and four feet tall, right on to the beam. I steered half into the sea, which gave us a bit more comfort. There were hundreds of craft in sight—open fishing boats, Tjalks under ruddy brown sails, commercial barges, fly bridge motor cruisers, expensive yachts, even a schooner. After half an hour or so, we headed back into the harbour of Hindeloope to re-join the inland system. As we tied up outside the lock, the harbour master came to tell us we were too large to get through this particular canal. Another peer at the chart showed that the next available port of entry was at Stavoren, some 12km further south, so we headed to sea once more. The passage took just over two hours, again heading slightly west of the course to avoid the worst of the rolling.

On the approach a large commercial came steaming out of the northern entrance. He was on our port side and the bearing was steady: we were on a collision course. In theory it was our right of way. Whether inland commercials didn't comply with the rules or whether there was an unwritten law that everybody gave way to commercials, I don't know. There was no way he was going to give way to us. He ploughed on regardless, and discretion and valour were words that came to mind as I eased off and passed around his stern. From Stavoren the canal opened out into the Fluessen, a wide expanse of water, with the channel marked by buoys. At Sneek (pronounced Snake), we moored beneath the picturesque Water Gate (no connection with Mr Nixon as far as I know). Sneek is a yachting paradise and haven for boats using the expansive Sneekermeer, and we were lucky to find such an excellent mooring—exactly long enough after a little help from our friends on a rented cruiser who moved up a couple of feet. We got talking to Gilles in a bar. Gilles was a bit of a forlorn character with a world-weary face. He wore a leather jacket and faded jeans. An ageing hippy probably aged in his late fifties, he told us he worked as a dogsbody for a local shipyard and had once built his own boat. He was very interested in our trip and talked about his plans.

He came to have a look at Saul Trader the next day with his girlfriend. Gilles had been married a couple of times before and had a daughter who lived in Arnhem. When I offered him a beer, his girlfriend intervened, and I got the impression that Gilles had to have his consumption restricted to save him from himself. He was a nice, gentle bloke, the sort of lost soul you meet holed up in boatyards, usually living in a battered mobile home at the back. He was a man who, like many, had seen his dreams washed away. We left Sneek and Gilles appeared from a shed in the boatyard and waved. As we disappeared out of sight he was still standing there in his overalls, roll-up in hand, lost in thoughts of distant dreams. I felt a little pang of sadness. That could easily have been me; it could have been any one of us.

The canal opened into the vast inland lake known as the Sneekermeer. It was filled with pleasure craft of all shapes and sizes, mixing with 1,000-tonners. It amazed me to see anglers sitting at anchor in tiny open boats just yards from the main channel, oblivious to the presence of huge commercials forging past just yards away. It also demonstrated how the Dutch fully embrace their waterways. We turned off the main channel at Terherne. There were so many waterway routes around there and we were spoilt for choice. I hadn't really planned a destination but the time to think about it more seriously was approaching fast. We had only a few more days before we were due to return to England. The broad idea was to keep heading roughly south east and possibly leave the boat in Meppel or Zwolle.

We found ourselves on the Herenveense Kanaal and stopped for the night in the unattractive town, eating on board. To get into the town arm we had to pass under an unmanned railway lift bridge. After our experiences at Leiden and Amsterdam, I'd been more than a bit apprehensive with lift bridges, especially unmanned railway ones. In the event we passed without incident. There was a button to press to indicate one's presence and after a wait of about ten minutes, during which time two trains sped by, the light flashed, and the bridge duly rose. Our route south of Herenveen was blocked by a low bridge, entailing roof lowering. It was raining hard, so I decided to take a different route which took us via the small and pleasant Stroomkanaal and then the Nieuwe Vaart, which joined the Dienste once more south of Assen, and would therefore complete our circle of Friesland.

The cruising was quiet and secluded and passed through pastures and small villages. We were in what was known as the Turf Route, a network of narrow canals built in the 19th century to transport peat. It was late August and the bridge keepers already seemed to be on the winter opening schedule. This meant they finished at 5pm, so progress was slow. We just missed the bridge at Gorredyck where I'd decided to try to leave the boat for a few weeks. The bridge keeper was extremely friendly and showed us an excellent mooring. His English was limited, and I tried to get over that I'd like to leave the boat for several weeks. Later in the day, the local canal secretary arrived to tell me that the canal would be closed from September 15th until the following May! He was very apologetic and said they were continually pressuring the authorities to extend the season. He presented us with a Turf Route window sticker, which to this day still graces a side window in the wheelhouse. We were two days from the Dienste, which meant that we would have to leave Gorredyck by September 13th. We would have to return in less than two weeks.

Most sensible people organise their winter moorings months, if not years, in advance. I rarely knew where I was going to end up and therefore arrangements in this regard were all rather last minute. Gorredyck had no rail connection and so we taxied back to collect the car from Assen. I returned on the 13th with Malcolm and my stepson Mark. The plan was to go back to Cambrai. The route was to be Arnhem and S'Hertogenbosch into Belgium and Herentals, the Albert Canal as far as Viersel, dive down through Brussels and the Ronquières inclined lane, descend the new lift at Strepy Thieu and then take the Canal de Centre into France and winter in the dead arm. What could be simpler!

The first couple of days to the junction with the Dienst passed uneventfully. At Uffelte we were held up involuntarily as the canal was closed for Sunday. There was little to do. The sun was warm, and we spent the time splashing about in the dinghy and catching up on some cleaning and polishing. Back on the river Ijssel we were now heading against the current, and it was a tortuous slog. It was at this point that the reason for the upstream boat instigating the blue board passing suddenly dawned on me. I noticed a crane barge ahead, blue boarding on left-hand bends. This meant he could hold the inside, which was obviously a shorter route and where the current had less effect. I followed suit which saved a lot of time, and we overnighted at Deventer. When we arrived, there was one commercial on the wall at least 100m long. We tied up, went ashore and found a pub with excellent Guinness, and went onto a first-class Indian restaurant. Life was not so bad. I was brought down to earth when we returned to the boat. Another eight or nine commercials had arrived, and I got a deserved admonishment (I wouldn't go so far as to call it a bollocking) from the skipper of the commercial tied up behind me. He said I should not have tied in the middle of the wall as I had effectively taken up two spaces; there was no room for a commercial between my bow and the end of the wall. Fair comment, and a mistake I never made again.

Next day we called at Zutphen for fuel and moored for the night at Arnhem, this time on the river Nederrhin in the centre of town. The reason there was space was there was a sluis closed on the canal, and all traffic was having to use the mighty Waal. This knowledge was not conducive to a relaxing evening. I'd wanted to take the much quieter Nederrhin as far as Rijswyck, then cut across to join the Waal at Tiel. The closure meant we would be on the Waal for something like 80km. Downstream it's true, but not a prospect I relished with the diesel in the state it was. I checked the small gauze filter in the hand prime pump and cleaned out some gunge. At that stage there was nothing more that I could do.

We cast off at 8am and nervously made our way back on to the Ijssel to head for the Waal, the waterway equivalent of the M25. As is often the case, the deed wasn't as bad as the thought. It was fast and furious, busy and choppy. We were doing 14kph most of the way. At times I counted more than 20 vessels in sight; some coming up on their correct side, some blue boarding and some crashing up from behind. Some were piled high with containers. I counted roughly one hundred on some of them, and huge ocean-going tugs pushing four massive dumb barges. There were others with wheelhouses perched high above the cargo on hydraulic posts which were lowered automatically by sensors as they approached a low bridge. Among this bedlam we even passed an Englishman on a narrowboat! Well, it's a free world—especially in Holland.

Our board was in and out like a fiddler's elbow. It was nothing if not exhilarating. There was hardly time to worry, although the thought of the engine suddenly sputtering to a halt was never far from my mind and bow and stern anchors were on standby. We flashed past massive shipyards, and Nijmegen came and went. We counted off the kilometres on the posts as they passed with remarkable speed. The junction with the Rijnkanaal where we would have joined the Waal from my preferred route skipped by and then we were looking out for the left turn into the connecting Kanaal van Sint Andries to take us into the Maas and the shelter of S'Hertogenbosch. The turn was tricky; three close behind us and another three ploughing upstream towards us. It was a question of calculating and anticipating and then going for it. One of the following boats turned in behind us and suddenly we were out of the maelstrom and under the lee of the lock gate. The Maas was positively tame by comparison and we were soon inside the huge lock, where Mick had found the very nice lady a few months earlier. It was nice to be back on the cut. We returned to Belgium by the same route we had taken in the spring, via Weert and the Zuid Willemsvaart Kanal to Herentals. No music festivals this time, and Mark left by train for home, so it was down to me and Malcolm.

Chapter 12

Cambrai Via The Belgian Lifts

I T WAS a Saturday morning when Malcolm and I dropped down the lock and entered the Albert Canal. We waited for a small English barge creeping up behind. During the entire descent, the husband shouted abuse at his wife. I wondered whether she was the instigator of a series of articles that appeared in the Dutch Barge Journal: he nice and dry in the wheelhouse, while she was on the foredeck soaked to the skin, the boat 12ft from the bank and he screaming at her to 'jump, you stupid bitch'.

It was gloomy and there was a depressing misty drizzle. I thought it would be reasonably quiet and was completely wrong—the canal was heaving. It was the main thoroughfare from the Rhine into Antwerp. The maximum size for vessels was about 3,500 tons and it seemed as though everything that was moving was of maximum dimensions. The distance from Herentals to the left turn at Viesel was 12km. After 5km, almost halfway, and having been passed both ways by about 70,000 tons of inland shipping, I started to relax a little. The sides were formed of sloping concrete walls with a ledge at the bottom about a foot wide. These caused the passing wash to hit three or four times as it bounced off. It was certainly no place to breakdown.

Then we broke down. My heart sank like a stone as the engine stuttered to a stop and we drifted helplessly in the swell. There were two more vessels ploughing up from behind and another heading towards us. I tried to use the bow thruster to edge us into the side, while Malcolm took a rope and made a precarious leap onto the ledge. It was wet and slippery. I called out for him to only try to stop the boat until the weigh had come off completely. I was worried about him being dragged into the canal. After a few more minutes the boat slowed until it was just about stopped, but it was still banging up and down quite violently as the big ones surged past, oblivious to our predicament. I managed to get off with a stern line. It was extremely difficult to get to the top of the slope, especially with a rope in one hand and a lively 60 tons on the other end. It was a case of crawling on hands and knees. Mr Abusive sailed haughtily past. I tried to indicate our plight by means of the hand sawing across the throat motion, but he took no notice, perhaps unfamiliar with the international code of sign language. 'Sod you then,' I yelled.

We got the boat loosely tied, one end to a lamppost and the other on to a stake. What now? I stood in the wheelhouse feeling pretty desperate. I really didn't want to have to get the filter out of the lift pump in this swell. I called my brother, as much for finding someone to share my plight with as for any real practical advice. After all, what could he do back in England? He might as well have been in the Antipodes. During our conversation I idly turned the ignition key and the engine burst into life. 'Let's go!' I yelled to Malcolm, and we frantically retrieved our ropes. Anything seemed better than staying where we were, and we made another kilometre before it died again. We spent a couple more minutes drifting, and with another few turns on the key we were away again. This way we made faltering progress towards the turning at Viersel, the turning that would give us an escape from these lumping boiling waters. Eventually I could see what looked like the entrance to the Nete through the binoculars. We had about a kilometre to go.

Right at the entrance there was a lock. I could see the outline of the control cabin and the opening where we would have to turn. As it was on the left it meant, of course, that we had to cross the channel while avoiding speeding traffic—a nightmare scenario in itself. A kilometre or so behind us another loaded 3,500-tonner forged its way towards us. I dare not turn across its path. The engine had been running for about ten minutes and by the law of averages was due to stop at any moment. If we became stranded sideways across the channel in front of him, the resulting impact didn't bear thinking about. I slowed down and waited. It seemed a ridiculously long time before the huge commercial crashed by and then there was a good clear run. We went for it… and then I made another mistake.

In my panic to get across I went far too close to the stern of the passing vessel and we were thrown violently from side to side in his wash. There was an almighty crash from below. There was no time to investigate that, as we were hanging on to stop being thrown over ourselves. I managed to steer for the shelter of the lock. Even inside, we still bounced up and down at least three or four feet before the top gates finally closed behind us and the waters calmed. The lock keeper gave us a wry smile. 'No place for small ships,' I said, and added under my breath, 'especially ones with a dodgy fuel supply.'

Below the lock it was like heaven; flat, smooth water and very little moving traffic. The engine stopped another three or four times, but I let it drift gently in the middle until eventually it roared back into life. At Lier there was a long floating pontoon with water and electricity, a small and welcome respite. We secured the boat and I immediately went below to dismantle the lift pump. There were six small Phillips screws that held the casing to the side of the engine, and it was all too easy to drop them into the bilge. Halfway through this exercise, Malcolm called down from the wheelhouse. 'Wedding party on board!' 'What the **** ?' 'Wedding party—want to know if it's OK to take photographs on board.'

I went aloft blinking in the late afternoon sun. What the hell was he on about? I thought the excitement had gone to his head, but sure enough there on the foc'sle stood a beautiful bride with her new husband and young escorts flashing their molars for the camera. Where they had appeared from, we hadn't a clue. There wasn't a church for miles. We could only assume they'd been driving to the reception and spotted the boat. 'You couldn't have written the script,' I said to Malcolm, diving back below for my camera. This was a scene I just had to record for posterity!

The engine still wouldn't start, even after the filter had been cleaned. It was dragging in air somewhere and I eventually traced it to one of the connectors. The thread had softened with so much use and would not tighten properly. It was getting towards evening and there was nothing I could do until morning, so we both showered and set off to have a look around Lier, a wonderful little town. Although it was a 25-minute walk to the centre, it was well worth it. Lier was a mini Bruges, surrounded by small waterways and beautiful buildings but without the grockels. In the Café Ste Gummaris, we asked whether there was anywhere we could see the England versus Slovakia football match (we hadn't forgotten the priorities despite everything). The Belgian barman replied in a thick and colloquial Irish accent. Leonard had spent two years in Galway and learned the language exactly, right down to 'so it was' and 'to be sure'. The bar was owned by two girls, Connie and Tine, and we became regulars for a few days. Tine's boyfriend was production manager at a Pringles factory and one evening he tried to explain how they got the crinkly curve affect but I'm afraid I switched off. He put us on to a small engineering firm who made up a length of pipe to do the job on Saul Trader until I could get the parts in England. I reconnected it the following day and the engine burst into life. A caretaker who looked after the mooring pontoon had arranged for a fuel tanker to deliver to several boats, so we took advantage and took on another 300 gallons. I reckoned that the higher the level in the tank, the less chance there was of the bug getting through the intake, although I don't think that theory was ever proved.

We were both just about bushed by now—no stamina, I suppose—and we decided to leave the boat for a few weeks and go home. It was the end of September and another couple of weeks would get us to Cambrai, fuel bug permitting. And just the two of us—myself and Malcolm, my trusty lookout—returned for the next leg. A shame, as we'd be experiencing two of the most interesting pieces of canal engineering in Europe, possibly the world: the Ronquières inclined plane and the new boat lift at Strepy Thieu, which had opened a few weeks earlier to replace the ancient boat lifts at Houdeng. But I was still worried about the engine stopping, and the unease took the edge off the enjoyment.

We dropped down the lock at Lier. The chart showed several entrances into the Brussels Canal and I intended taking the first available. Just before we reached this, I noticed two telltale signs. Our speed had noticeably increased and the glistening wet mud on the sloping sides told me something I should have already known… this river was tidal! Yet again, I was unprepared. I hadn't a clue as to the rise and fall or the times of high and low water. Then, as we approached what the chart showed to be a lock at Boom, it slowly became apparent that this lock was well and truly closed. Another 10km at the mercy of the tide before the next entrance, at Rupelmonde, back on the Schelde; 10km I could well have done without. It was a great relief to finally turn left at the junction with the Schelde and see the open gates of the huge lock.

I don't dislike rivers at all. In fact I love the fresh smell of the weirs and the moving water, but when you have the constant worry of the engine letting you down and you are always listening subconsciously for the dreaded faltering beat, it is not so much fun. The lock keeper waved us right to the far end of the lock. That meant only one thing—more vessels on the way, and sure enough we were soon joined by two giant container ships.

Some four or five kilometres above the lock we stopped for the night at Willebroek, where Mrs Bradshaw recommended a good basic and reasonably priced restaurant. We moored directly above the closed lock we'd passed on the river which, had it been operating, would have saved us 20km and nearly five hours! From our position we could see it was being completely restored. There is a statue here to the Bateliers, and the restaurant recommended by Mrs B had changed hands and become a fashionable Italian. After the meal, we were treated to a display of fireworks from Boom on the opposite bank of the Rupel, before heading back to the boat for a peaceful night... but not such a peaceful morning. At 6am we were woken by the shouts of workmen and the hammering ring of the pneumatic drill. We were in the way of something or other and had to move. There was nowhere else suitable to tie up, so we kept going.

We passed through the impressive lifting bridge in pouring rain, through Tisselt and through a grey and uninviting outskirts of Brussels, to the pretty little town of Halle, where we moored to a trip boat landing stage, close to the centre, having ascertained that the trips had finished for the season. Two things stand out in my memory about Halle, an otherwise fairly nondescript sort of place. The first was being offered the (very drunk) barmaid for the night by the (even more drunk) barman, and the second, much more exciting, was standing on the platform of the recently and superbly modernised station to watch the Eurostars rush through on their way to and from Brussels. The Ronquières inclined plane is an engineering masterpiece, built in 1968, raising boats 220ft inside a trough on an inclined track 1,432m (nearly a mile) long. We had to wait at the bottom for two and a half hours as there was only one tank operating. There was a distinct air of dissent among the bateliers; it seemed rather ridiculous that having finally opened the new lift, providing access from the Schelde to the Meuse for larger vessels and thereby substantially increasing traffic, that the authorities should deem it necessary to have only one caisson operating. The complete cycle took two hours and each caisson has a capacity for just one 1,350-tonner. At the next turn there were three 600-tonners in the queue, and when the first two were in it was obvious there wouldn't be enough room for the third.

Without waiting to be asked I put Saul Trader in behind the second one. I found that if there was space, then go for it. It was the same procedure for locks. I didn't use the VHF very much but the éclusiers would soon let you know if they didn't want you in their lock, either by switching the light to red or simply shutting the gate in your face. In the main they were only too happy to let you in and avoid unnecessary waste of time and water. The other thing I learned from experience was that the commercials took an age to get positioned in a lock. I once made the mistake of going in too soon behind one and got caught in his wash as he manoeuvred his stern alongside. We were dragged into the vortex and smacked quite hard into his stern, which didn't exactly endear us to him. Now I followed their example and crept slowly in. This gave far more control when reversing to stop. The early tendency is to panic and worry that you are holding them all up but it's far from that and much better to do things in a controlled and orderly manner. You have far more control over the movement of the boat going astern when you're going slowly. Prop-walk, as it's known, is the effect of the stern of the boat when going backwards. If the vessel is moving too quickly through the water, the steerer has little or no control as to where the stern will go. Coming alongside is so much easier when the movement is controlled down to a very slow crawl. Most beginners think they should do everything at breakneck speed, which is the cause of the majority of embarrassing mishaps.

The ascent of the Ronquières lift took 25 minutes, during which we got off the boat and wandered about on the side deck of the caisson. The operator travelled with us, driving from a small cabin. The weather was misty and dull, a pity as the view from the top would have been worth a photograph or two. Amazingly there was no charge for the ride. At the top there was an excellent visitor centre and exhibition which we'd visited on a previous occasion and was well worth the small entrance fee. There was also a viewing tower providing fantastic views of the lift and the surrounding countryside.

It seemed incredible that in a little over 20km, the new multi-million Euro boat lift would take us back down to the level we'd left at the bottom of the plane. We arrived at the top of the lift at dusk and entered behind two small French péniches. This lift also took 1,350-tonners and with the two Frenchmen, our combined tonnage was about 750. The vital statistics were mind boggling. The lift could raise and lower boats 73m (240ft) in just seven minutes. The caissons, at 112m long and 12m wide, were each supported by 112 cables 85mm in diameter. Four electric motors powered eight winches for each caisson. It took 20 years to build and cost 160-million Euros. We were charged one Euro and five cents for the ride, although I believe this charge was later dropped altogether. Equally amazing, for my money, was the giant aqueduct some 5km long that had to be constructed to link up with original line of the canal. It carried these huge vessels high in the air, crossing a busy motorway in the process. This had, in fact, been the most difficult part of the work and, for both logistical and financial reasons, had caused the long delay in finishing the project.

With typical logic, the only way to get to the office to pay was by crossing the end gates. To do this you had to pass a chained-up gate with the words Access Interdit boldly emblazoned on it. I received an invoice (facture) for this service, stating Saul Trader was categorised as a Type 91, with maximum tonnage at 0060 and marchandaise 0000. Passengers were curiously 0000 and Conteiners oooo. All of this was neatly typed out by computer and all for the Forfait of 87 Eurocents plus 18 cents TVP (VAT to you and me!). As I crossed over the mezzanine walkway at the 'open' end, I was amazed that I could look down through a gap to the bottom—240ft below.

Another long day saw us into France, and we shared the lock at Fresne sur L'Escaut with two pairs of push-tow péniches. For extra capacity they would connect two 350-ton boats together in line, creating an unwieldy vessel 5m wide and 76m long—a modern-day narrowboat pair I suppose! By the time we left the lock it was pitch black and the éclusier directed us to a staging where we tied up for the night. It was 9pm.

Fresne was a small and slightly grubby little town. I didn't hold out much hope for food, but we hadn't much on board. The first bar we found was just about to close but they pointed us to a little takeaway where we settled for burgers and chips smothered in mayonnaise. As we strolled back along the main street my eye was caught by a display in the window of a rundown toy shop. I couldn't believe my eyes. There were boxes of Hornby Acho model trains! Without wishing to bore you, Hornby Acho was the French equivalent of Hornby Dublo, which ceased production in 1964 when the old Meccano company went bust. I'd collected Hornby trains for many years and here was what looked like every collector's dream. A dusty toy shop with some original stock; the prices were still marked in Francs! Orgasmic! I was like the little boy in a sweet shop. I told Malcolm that we wouldn't be leaving too early in the morning.

As it turned out, all was not exactly as it appeared. The shop was full of old stock and was run by a dear old lady who must have been aged in her upper eighties and who talked incessantly, in French, totally oblivious to the fact we couldn't understand a bloody word. She insisted on lifting her leg on to the counter—no mean feat either at her age—to show us her ulcerated ankle and explain she had to go to the doctor but would be back in half an hour. The trains, she explained, were being sold on behalf of a customer who had priced it himself. We struck a bargain and for 600 Euros I came away with two very large boxes of trains. I think both sides were reasonably satisfied with the deal.

On the last day to Cambrai it rained continually. Malcolm stood dutifully at his post on the bow as we negotiated lock after lock, and he was soaked to the skin. You had to hand it to Malcolm. He was a tough little bugger. He'd been standing on the foredeck tending the lines for four hours and I never heard him complain once. We raced on to get through the last lock before it closed at before 6pm. At one lock I bought a bag of potatoes from the éclusier, much to Malcolm's amusement, on the promise he would call the next lock (the last one before Cambrai) to ensure it was ready for us. We just made it with minutes to spare and turned right into the dead arm at Cambrai at exactly six.

The next morning, we ran the engine and hosed down the decks. When we'd finished, I switched off the engine and immediately noticed a strong smell of diesel. When I went into the engine room to investigate, I immediately saw the problem. The cork gasket on the made-up bit of pipe from Lier had disintegrated and for the last hour or so had been squirting a fine jet of diesel into the bilge. Sod it, I thought, I'm not clearing it up now—it'll have to wait until the spring. It was against my better nature to leave it, but we'd both had enough, and we had a ferry to catch. It wouldn't do any harm.

We finished clearing up the cabins. I had made a check list of shutdown procedures I meticulously followed. The first was: Close down fresh water tank valves. That was one hassle I didn't want again!

Acknowledgements

THANK YOU to everyone who accompanied me on these trips. I consider myself lucky to have known so many colourful characters.

I have tried to describe everyone accurately and portray them in a true and entertaining way. I sincerely hope I have not offended anyone; if so, I apologise unreservedly. The names of the characters in this book have not been changed in order to implicate the guilty.

Finally, a big thanks to Allen Maslen, who has guided me through the sometimes painful process of being published.

About The Author

KEITH HARRIS was born and brought up in Hastings, beside the sea and many miles from the nearest navigable canal.

It was not until 1976 that he hired his first narrowboat—and he was hooked. Keith had always had a keen interest in railways and canals held the same fascination. He bought his first narrowboat in 1984 and got the chance to buy the replica Dutch Luxemotor, Saul Trader, in 1998. He still owns both boats and gets the same 'kick' when he goes aboard after an absence.

The lore of the cut has stayed with him and will do so forever.

Keith now lives in Wiltshire. He spends several months of the year on the boats or travelling around the world.

The adventures of the Saul Trader in this book took place in 2001. British Waterways has since been superseded by the Canal and River Trust.